Dear Jennifer,
Hope you enjoy
these recipes as
much as we have.
Love,
Mehraz + Ned
Christmas 2007

# Savoring Sandestin

Recipes and Memories
From Sunrise to Sunset

*All proceeds from the sale of* Savoring Sandestin *will benefit*
*Sacred Heart Hospital on the Emerald Coast.*

Published by Sandestin Golf and Beach Resort

*Savoring Sandestin*

Copyright 2002 by
Sandestin Golf and Beach Resort
9300 Emerald Coast Parkway West
Sandestin, Florida 32550
1-800-277-0801

This cookbook is a collection of favorite recipes,
which are not necessarily original recipes.

Library of Congress Catalog Number: 2002092255
ISBN: 0-9718138-0-9

Edited, Designed, and Manufactured by
Favorite Recipes® Press
an Imprint of

FRP

P.O. Box 305142
Nashville, Tennessee 37230
800-358-0560

Art Director: Steve Newman
Book Design: Brad Whitfield and Susan Breining
Project Managers: Elizabeth Mohlenkamp and Tanis Westbrook

Manufactured in the United States of America
First Printing: 2002
20,000 copies

We are overwhelmed at the enthusiastic and total support this endeavor generated.
First of all, much credit goes to Sandestin owner Ginger Lundstrom who
conceived the idea of compiling a book of Sandestin owners' recipes as a vehicle to
benefit a local charity. Little did we know at that time how this project would grow!
When we needed more funding, Sandestin Resort willingly expanded
our budget (thank you Mike Stange and Jim Boivin!).

The glorious Sandestin photographs came from several sources, but we owe a major
debt to Allison Yii, who opened up the complete Sandestin archives to us, and to
Libby Edmonds, whose beautiful photo provided the inspiration for our cover.
Sandestin owner and book committee member Joan Gough was involved from the
beginning and contributed so much in talent and hours. Peggy Sue Mullins spent
days bent over slides helping us go through the thousands of available photos.

We are grateful to Sacred Heart Hospital on the Emerald Coast for inspiring this book
and bringing much-needed services to this little bit of paradise. Our publisher,
Favorite Recipes Press, is clearly responsible for the beautiful book you hold now.
The FRP staff inspired us with their talent, skill, and patience. Finally, we are thankful
to the people who made this journal of recipes and memories possible—
the owners, residents, and chefs of Sandestin Resort. We were amazed at the
generous outpouring and sharing of ideas, recipes, and stories.
This book is truly your gift to our community.

*Peggy Brown    Deborah Hale*
*Editors*

# Contents

# Contents

# A Hearty Welcome

Sandestin is a feast for the senses. Whether it is the rhythmic waves lapping along our spectacular sugar white beaches, or the soft mist rolling off the green fairways giving way to another sunny day at our 2,400-acre resort. Whether it is the delighted squeals from children playing on Jolee Island, or the shared laughter of friends remembering adventures of the past day at a Village café. Whatever the moment captured, the sights and sounds of Sandestin offer a sense of warmth and comfort.

The feelings that Sandestin inspires can be difficult to describe at times, but those who have discovered this paradise will tell you that one thing is easily understood—Sandestin is a place to call home. As the resort home for so many kind and gracious people, Sandestin is often a special place for family and friends to gather together. It is a place where traditions are born and kept; where family memories are made and treasured. So, we thought it would be only appropriate that we celebrate our families and share our stories by creating a Sandestin family cookbook.

On these pages, you'll find the hospitality of our fine homeowners extended to you through their personal family recipes. The memorable meals you'll make will be secondary to the fascinating people you'll discover with every tasty new dish you try. Each chapter will welcome you into a new neighborhood and each page you turn will take you further into exploring the most spectacular resort in North America. As you stimulate your senses and sample these treasured recipes, we hope that they help you to create your own unique memories of Sandestin, where everyone is family and hospitality is a way of life.

We offer our heartfelt thanks to everyone who gave of their time and talents to make this project possible. And our appreciation is extended to you, the reader, for making Sandestin a part of your hearth and home.

With this project, we serve up our support to Sacred Heart Hospital, which will enjoy proceeds from each Sandestin cookbook sold. We are proud to have such a fine and valuable institution in our community and wish them every success. Be well and enjoy.

*Mike Stange*
Vice President, General Manager
Sandestin Golf and Beach Resort

# Thanks to You, We're Really Cookin'...

On behalf of the residents and visitors to the Destin area, Sacred Heart Hospital
on the Emerald Coast extends our sincere thanks for your purchase of
*Savoring Sandestin.*

While you may have simply purchased the book for the great recipes,
we want you to know that your purchase has actually helped underwrite
the costs of providing quality health care to any and all who are in need of it
at the beautiful new Sacred Heart Hospital on the Emerald Coast.

Thanks to the generosity of Sandestin Golf and Beach Resort—who paid all
production and promotion costs for this book—100 percent of the proceeds from
your purchase was directly donated to Sacred Heart Hospital on the Emerald Coast.
Initially, your donation helped to construct this wonderful resource for
our community. Upon completion of construction (December 2002),
donations will help to contribute to the expansion of services as well as helping
to underwrite the costs of health care for those in our area who do not have
the means to pay for it themselves.

We hope you will enjoy this delicious assortment of recipes, stories, and snippets of
life in Sandestin. As you savor your very favorites from this unique collection,
we are certain that the knowledge that your purchase of this book is
helping those in need will also feed your soul.

*Patrick J. Madden, FACHE*
President and CEO

# History

The name of our resort community, Sandestin Resort, is a fusion of the names of the two towns that border it on either side—Santa Rosa Beach and Destin.

The first known residents in our area were the Native Americans about 12,000 years ago, when Florida was a wilderness. The Native Americans who peopled the Gulf of Mexico and the river valley that eventually became Choctawhatchee Bay were mound dwellers who established their communities along our area waters. Archaeological evidence of some of these settlements has been found on Sandestin and has been preserved.

Since the early 1500s, white men have come and gone along the Emerald Coast. The Spanish, French, and English have all left their indelible marks upon the face of the land. Indeed, over five centuries, five different flags have flown here— the Spanish, French, British, the stars and bars of the Confederacy, and the stars and stripes of the United States.

The natural bounty of the Emerald Coast has always captured the dreams of people who come here. Sandestin Resort first opened in 1974 with just a few hundred acres, a Sheraton Hotel (where the Bay Club is now located), the Links golf course, and a grass hut on the beach.

Well-known names appear in Sandestin's history. The first recorded owner of the property we now call Sandestin Resort was Mr. Bushnell, Attorney General of Massachusetts, who bought the land in 1930 for the purpose of raising crops and livestock.

Upon his death, the land transferred in ownership to his sister, Mrs. Coffeen.
She sold most of the land to a member of the Rockefeller family, Winthrop Rockefeller
of Little Rock, Arkansas. His plans for the property included a beach neighborhood
to be named "Forest-by-the-Sea." His grand ideas for developing our area
were sidetracked when he was elected governor of Arkansas.

We can thank Mrs. Coffeen that our pristine community did not become a raceway.
The owner of the Indianapolis Motor Speedway attempted to buy the Rockefeller
and Coffeen parcels in 1970, but Mrs. Coffeen refused to sell.

In the early 1970s, Evans and Mitchell Industries of Atlanta purchased the parcels,
and Sandestin was born. But Evans and Mitchell's involvement was short-lived.
The company lost the development to Chase Manhattan Trust who sold it to
Lakeland BV, a Dutch corporation owned by I.L.A. van Bohemen. Mr. van Bohemen
hired a young man named Peter Bos to manage the property and, in 1981,
Bos purchased Sandestin. Under the encouragement of Mr. van Bohemen and
the vision of Peter Bos, what we now know as Sandestin took shape.

In 1991, a British-Malaysian company called Sime Darby Berhad, one of
Southeast Asia's largest multinational conglomerates, purchased Sandestin.
In 1998, Intrawest, the leading developer and operator of mountain resorts
across North America, acquired Sandestin. The Village at Baytowne Wharf,
now the heart of the resort, was conceived as part of Intrawest's envisioning of
the future for Sandestin Resort.

# The White Sand Story

Ever wonder why our beaches have the whitest and the most homogenous sands in the world? Well, here is what the experts say . . .

The Apalachicola River, which is about 110 miles east of Sandestin Beach Resort, is possibly the most important factor controlling the special type of sand we find on our beaches today.

About twenty thousand years ago, the world witnessed the end of the last Ice Age, known as the Late Wisconsin. During the Wisconsin, voluminous amounts of water comprising the world's oceans were locked up in the great ice caps on the continents. Therefore, as one might expect, the sea level was at that time hundreds of feet below present-day sea level and the shoreline was displaced many miles offshore.

As the world temperatures began warming, the continental ice sheets began melting, thus providing large volumes of water that were subsequently carried by rivers to the world's oceans. The Apalachicola River, rising in the Appalachians, brought vast amounts of water to the Gulf of Mexico (and continues to do so today). Within this large volume of water were billions of small particles chemically weathered and eroded from the parent rock that comprises the Appalachian Mountains. For thousands of years, these small quartz particles were deposited offshore in the Gulf of Mexico in a delta, fan-type formation. Sea levels continued to rise rapidly and, in doing so, reworked these quartz grains across the continental shelf toward our present-day shoreline.

This process of reworking continued until around five thousand years ago, when the rate of sea level rise began to level off. At that time, our beaches began to form. The quartz-sand material, delivered to the Gulf of Mexico from the Appalachians via the Apalachicola River, was now being deposited along the shores.

From around five thousand years ago, our island began to extend from Destin like an arm. This extension continues today as these small, white quartz sands move incessantly to the west. So that's the story. No wonder Sandestin Beach Resort's beaches are so white; our sands are QUARTZ.

Sandestin at Sunrise

# Orange Smoothie

1 cup vanilla frozen yogurt
¼ cup low-fat milk
¼ cup orange juice
1 banana (optional)
6 to 8 ice cubes

Combine the yogurt, milk, orange juice, banana and ice cubes in a blender and process until smooth. Pour into chilled glasses and serve.

*Yield: 2 servings*

# Fruit Smoothie

1 very ripe banana
1 cup fresh fruit, such as strawberries, cranberries or
    peach slices
1 cup skim milk
2 or 3 ice cubes

Combine the banana, fruit, milk and ice cubes in a blender and process until smooth. Pour into chilled glasses and serve.

*Yield: 2 servings*

# Breakfast Smoothie

1 cup plain yogurt
1 tablespoon honey, or to taste
4 or 5 ice cubes, crushed
1/2 to 1 cup orange juice
1 to 2 bananas
Fresh peach slices, blueberries or strawberries to taste

Combine the yogurt, honey, crushed ice, orange juice, bananas and fresh fruit in a blender and process until smooth. Pour into chilled glasses and serve.

*Yield: 2 to 3 servings*

## A Recipe of Memories

1 beachside wedding
1 dozen crazy Christmases
2 beach chairs
1 dash of saltwater
1 cup of sand

*Mix all the ingredients together and you get a collection of priceless memories.*

*Jim and Donna McKern were married in 1990 at the Elephant Walk. They, and now their children, have created fabulous traditions at the beach, both in the summer and at Christmas. At Christmas, they decorate the tree with the tackiest of lights and ridiculous ornaments. They get the kids in the spirit by convincing them to don crazy Christmas Eve pajamas. Donna says that Sandestin has always been their getaway destination, but that it got harder and harder to leave. So, now Sandestin is their year-round home.*

# Monkey Bread

1/2 cup sugar

1 teaspoon cinnamon

3 (10-count) cans refrigerated biscuits

Sugar

1 teaspoon cinnamon

1/2 cup (1 stick) butter or margarine, melted

Combine 1/2 cup sugar and 1 teaspoon cinnamon in a bowl and mix well. Cut each biscuit into quarters and roll in the cinnamon mixture to coat. Layer in a buttered bundt pan. Pour any remaining cinnamon mixture into a measuring cup. Add enough sugar to measure 1 cup. Pour into a bowl. Add 1 teaspoon cinnamon and the melted butter and mix well. Spoon over the prepared layers in the pan. Bake at 350 degrees for 30 minutes. Cool slightly. Invert onto a serving plate.

*Note:* You may reduce this recipe by 1/3, using 2 cans of biscuits. Bake at 375 degrees for 22 minutes.

*Yield: 12 to 15 servings*

# Overnight Coffee Cake

1 (16-ounce) package frozen dinner rolls

1 (4-ounce) package butterscotch instant pudding mix

1 cup packed brown sugar

2 tablespoons cinnamon

1/2 cup (1 stick) butter, melted

1/2 cup chopped pecans

Layer the rolls, pudding mix, brown sugar, cinnamon, butter and pecans in the order listed in a greased bundt pan. Cover the pan with foil. Cover the foil with a kitchen towel. Let stand at room temperature overnight. Bake, uncovered, at 350 degrees for 30 minutes. Cool slightly. Invert onto a serving plate.

*Yield: 16 servings*

# Sour Cream Coffee Cake

½ cup (1 stick) butter or margarine, softened

1 cup sugar

2 cups flour

1 teaspoon baking powder

1 teaspoon baking soda

1 teaspoon salt

2 eggs

1 cup sour cream

1 teaspoon vanilla extract

½ cup sugar

2 teaspoons cinnamon

½ cup chopped nuts

Cream the butter and 1 cup sugar in a large mixing bowl until light and fluffy. Sift the flour, baking powder, baking soda and salt together. Add the eggs, sour cream and vanilla to the creamed mixture and mix well. Beat in the sifted dry ingredients. Combine ½ cup sugar, the cinnamon and nuts in a bowl and mix well.

Pour ⅓ of the batter into a greased tube pan. Sprinkle with ⅓ of the cinnamon mixture. Layer with ½ of the remaining batter and a little more than ½ of the remaining cinnamon mixture. Top with the remaining batter and cinnamon mixture. Cut through the batter 1 inch from the center of the pan with a knife to marbleize. Bake at 350 degrees for 45 minutes. Cool in the pan for 10 minutes. Invert onto a serving plate.

*Yield: 16 servings*

# Cherry Pecan Coffee Cake

**PECAN TOPPING**

2 tablespoons margarine, softened

1/2 cup sugar

1/2 cup flour

1 teaspoon cinnamon

1/2 cup chopped pecans

**CHERRY COFFEE CAKE**

1/2 cup (1 stick) margarine, softened

1 cup sugar

2 eggs

1 cup sour cream

2 cups flour

1 1/2 teaspoons baking powder

1/2 teaspoon baking soda

1/2 teaspoon salt

1 teaspoon vanilla extract

1 (21-ounce) can cherry pie filling

*For the topping,* cream the margarine and sugar in a mixing bowl until light and fluffy. Add the flour, cinnamon and pecans and mix well.

*For the cake,* cream the margarine and sugar in a mixing bowl until light and fluffy. Add the eggs and sour cream and mix well. Sift the flour, baking powder, baking soda and salt together. Add to the egg mixture and mix well. Stir in the vanilla. Pour 1/2 of the batter into a greased and floured 9×13-inch cake pan. Spread the cherry pie filling evenly over the batter. Top with the remaining batter. Sprinkle the topping over the batter in the prepared pan. Bake at 350 degrees for 50 to 60 minutes or until the coffee cake tests done.

You may substitute blueberry or apple pie filling for the cherry pie filling. Add cinnamon to taste, if using apple pie filling.

*Yield: 15 servings*

# Low-Fat Cranberry Pumpkin Bread

3$1/2$ cups flour

1 cup packed brown sugar

2 teaspoons baking soda

1 teaspoon baking powder

$3/4$ teaspoon salt

1 teaspoon cinnamon

$1/2$ teaspoon ground cloves

1 cup egg substitute

1 (16-ounce) can whole cranberry sauce

1 (15-ounce) can solid-pack pumpkin, or

   2 cups mashed cooked sweet potatoes

$1/3$ cup vegetable oil or applesauce

1 tablespoon finely grated orange zest

2 tablespoons chopped nuts

Combine the flour, brown sugar, baking soda, baking powder, salt, cinnamon and cloves in a large bowl and mix well. Combine the egg substitute, cranberry sauce, pumpkin, oil and orange zest in a bowl and mix well. Pour into the flour mixture and mix just until moistened. Pour into two 4×8-inch loaf pans sprayed with nonstick cooking spray. Sprinkle evenly with the nuts. Bake at 350 degrees for 1 hour or until the loaves test done.

*Yield: 2 loaves*

## Memories

*Tina and John Burke vividly remember the first time they toured Sandestin. "It was raining so hard, we couldn't see out of the windows of the car," recalls Tina. Despite the "wet" reception, the Burkes became homeowners at Sandestin that weekend.*

# Blueberry Muffins

1 egg
3/4 cup milk
3 tablespoons vegetable oil
1 teaspoon vanilla extract
2 cups flour
3/4 cup sugar
2 teaspoons baking powder
1 teaspoon baking soda
1/2 teaspoon salt
1 cup blueberries
Confectioners' sugar to taste
Orange juice to taste

Combine the egg, milk, oil and vanilla in a large bowl and mix well. Whisk the flour, sugar, baking powder, baking soda and salt in a bowl. Add the flour mixture to the egg mixture and stir just until moistened. Fold in the blueberries. Spoon into greased muffin cups. Bake at 375 degrees for 25 minutes. Cool in the pan for 1 minute. Remove to a wire rack. Whisk the desired amount of confectioners' sugar and orange juice in a bowl to make a glaze. Drizzle over the warm muffins.

*Yield: 1 dozen muffins*

# Best Blueberry Muffins

## CINNAMON TOPPING

1/2 cup sugar

1/4 cup flour

1 teaspoon cinnamon

3 tablespoons chilled butter

## BLUEBERRY MUFFINS

1/2 cup (1 stick) butter, softened

1 cup sugar

2 eggs

1 teaspoon vanilla extract

2 cups flour

2 teaspoons baking powder

1/2 teaspoon salt

1/2 cup milk

2 1/2 cups fresh blueberries

**For the topping,** combine the sugar, flour and cinnamon in a bowl and mix well. Cut in the butter with a fork until crumbly.

**For the muffins,** spray 18 muffin cups with nonstick cooking spray. Line with paper baking cups. Cream the butter and sugar in a mixing bowl until light and fluffy. Add the eggs 1 at a time, beating well after each addition. Stir in the vanilla. Sift the flour, baking powder and salt together 2 times. Add to the creamed mixture alternately with the milk, mixing well after each addition.

Mash 1/2 cup of the blueberries in a bowl. Add to the batter and mix well. Fold in the remaining blueberries. Fill the prepared muffin cups 1/2 to 2/3 full. Sprinkle the topping evenly over the tops of the muffin batter. Bake at 375 degrees for 30 minutes. Serve hot.

*Yield: 18 muffins*

# Lavender Scones

## LAVENDER SCONES

3 cups self-rising flour
1/2 to 3/4 cup sugar
1 tablespoon ground fresh lavender

1/2 cup (1 stick) chilled butter,
    cut into pieces
3/4 cup buttermilk

## LAVENDER GLAZE

1 cup confectioners' sugar
2 to 3 tablespoons water
1/2 teaspoon powdered lavender
    (see note)

1 or 2 drops each of red and blue
    food coloring

*For the scones,* combine the self-rising flour, sugar and lavender in a bowl and mix well. Cut in the butter using a pastry blender until the mixture resembles coarse meal. Add the buttermilk and stir until a soft dough forms. Pat the dough 1 inch thick on a lightly floured surface. Cut with a small biscuit cutter. Arrange on a greased baking sheet. Bake at 400 degrees for 8 to 10 minutes or until light brown. Cool on the baking sheet.

*For the glaze,* combine the confectioners' sugar, water, lavender and food coloring in a bowl and mix until smooth. Drizzle over the scones and serve. Store leftovers in an airtight container. Wrap the scones in foil to reheat.

*Note:* Purchase edible culinary lavender and process the flower heads in a food processor until of a powder consistency. Store in a glass container and use as needed.

*Yield: 30 scones*

*Magnolia & Ivy Tearoom*

# Microwave Lemon Curd

*This makes a great condiment for scones.*

3 eggs
1/2 cup fresh lemon juice
1/2 cup (1 stick) butter, melted
1 cup sugar

Whisk the eggs in a microwave-safe bowl until frothy. Whisk in the lemon juice, butter and sugar until smooth. Microwave on High for 3 minutes. Whisk the mixture vigorously. Microwave on High for 3 minutes longer. Whisk the mixture vigorously. Repeat the process once more, if necessary, until the mixture begins to thicken. Store, covered, in the refrigerator for up to 2 weeks. Serve in a small crystal dish and garnish with a small fresh pansy or violet.

*Yield: (about) 2¹/₂ cups*

Magnolia & Ivy Tearoom

## Local Interest

The Sandestin area is well-known for its wildlife. The great blue heron and great white egret are full-time residents, but from spring to late fall they are joined by other members of the heron family: snowy egret, cattle egret, night heron, little blue heron, tri-colored heron, and sometimes, the reddish heron. All can be seen around the ponds, lakes, and bays, hunting for food. Watch carefully and you might see one trying to swallow a meal that looks too large for its long, narrow neck, but swallow it they do! Often fishermen on the pier off the Links Golf Course 13th hole will see a lazy great blue heron hanging around hoping a lucky angler will throw it a fish. Don't they know about the "catch and release" policy?

# Heart Healthy Beach Cookies

10 ounces Take Control vegetable oil spread (do not use light)
1 cup brown sugar (do not pack)
1 cup sugar
6 egg whites, lightly beaten
2 teaspoons vanilla extract
3 cups flour
2 teaspoons baking soda
2 teaspoons cinnamon
1 teaspoon salt
6 cups rolled oats
10 ounces chopped dates (optional)
1 to 2 cups chopped walnuts
1 to 2 cups chopped pecans

Cream the butter substitute, brown sugar and sugar in a mixing bowl until light and fluffy. Add the egg whites and vanilla and mix well. Sift the flour, baking soda, cinnamon and salt together. Add to the creamed mixture and mix well. Stir in the oats, dates, walnuts and pecans. Drop by tablespoonfuls 2 inches apart onto a cookie sheet sprayed with nonstick cooking spray. Bake at 365 degrees for 12 to 14 minutes. Cool on the cookie sheet for 1 minute. Remove to a wire rack to cool completely.

*Yield: 12 dozen cookies*

# Oatmeal Cookies

1 (2-layer) package spice cake mix
1/4 cup packed dark brown sugar
2 eggs
3/4 cup vegetable oil

1/2 cup milk
2 cups rolled oats
2 cups raisins
1 cup chopped nuts

Combine the cake mix, brown sugar, eggs, oil and milk in a large bowl and mix well. Stir in the oats, raisins and nuts. Drop by spoonfuls 2 inches apart onto an ungreased cookie sheet. Bake at 350 degrees for 12 minutes. Cool on the cookie sheet for 1 minute. Remove to a wire rack to cool completely.

*Yield: 4 dozen cookies*

# Cowboy Cookies

1 cup shortening
1 cup sugar
1 cup firmly packed light brown sugar
2 eggs
1 1/2 teaspoons vanilla extract
1 1/2 cups flour

1 teaspoon baking soda
1 teaspoon salt
3 cups quick-cooking oats
1 cup chopped pecans
1 cup (6 ounces) semisweet or dark
  chocolate chips

Cream the shortening, sugar and brown sugar in a mixing bowl until light and fluffy. Add the eggs 1 at a time, beating well after each addition. Beat in the vanilla. Sift the flour, baking soda and salt together. Add to the creamed mixture gradually, mixing well after each addition. Stir in the oats, pecans and chocolate chips. Drop by spoonfuls 2 inches apart onto a well-greased cookie sheet. Bake at 350 degrees for 10 minutes or until golden brown. Cool on the cookie sheet for 1 minute. Remove to a wire rack to cool completely. Store in an airtight container.

*Yield: 6 dozen cookies*

# Make-Ahead French Toast

1/2 cup (1 stick) butter, melted

1 cup packed dark brown sugar

1 French baguette, sliced

6 eggs

1 1/2 cups milk

1 teaspoon vanilla extract

Confectioners' sugar to taste

Warm pancake syrup

Combine the butter and brown sugar in a bowl and mix well. Pour into a 9×13-inch baking dish. Layer the bread slices over the butter mixture. Beat the eggs, milk and vanilla in a bowl until well blended. Pour over the bread slices. Refrigerate, covered, for 8 to 12 hours. Bake, uncovered, at 350 degrees for 45 minutes. Sprinkle with confectioners' sugar. Serve with warm pancake syrup.

*Yield: 8 to 10 servings*

# Michigan Blueberry Syrup

3/4 cup water

2 cups sugar

1 tablespoon lemon juice

2 teaspoons cornstarch

1 tablespoon water

2 teaspoons quick-cooking tapioca

1 cup fresh blueberries

Bring 3/4 cup water and the sugar to a boil in a saucepan over medium heat. Cook until the sugar dissolves, stirring constantly. Stir in the lemon juice. Combine the cornstarch and 1 tablespoon water in a small cup. Add to the sugar mixture. Cook over medium heat until clear and thickened, whisking constantly. Stir in the tapioca and blueberries. Cook for several minutes longer, stirring constantly. Cool slightly. Serve over pancakes, waffles or ice cream.

*Yield: (about) 2 1/2 cups*

# Breakfast Potatoes

1 pound bulk pork sausage or lean ground beef
Extra-virgin olive oil
10 to 15 new potatoes, thinly sliced
1 Vidalia onion, chopped
1/2 green bell pepper, chopped
1/2 red bell pepper, chopped
1/2 yellow bell pepper, chopped
Garlic salt to taste
Freshly ground pepper to taste
Shredded Cheddar cheese to taste (optional)

Brown the sausage in a skillet, stirring until crumbly; drain. Cover the bottom of a large skillet with olive oil and place over medium heat. Add the potatoes and cook for 15 to 20 minutes or until the potatoes begin to soften, stirring occasionally. Add the onion, bell peppers, sausage, garlic salt and pepper. Cook, covered, for 15 to 20 minutes or until the vegetables are done to taste. Sprinkle with cheese. Let stand until the cheese melts. Serve with fried eggs for a complete breakfast.

*Yield: 6 to 8 servings*

# Sunrise Fries

4 cups cooked hash brown potatoes
1 green bell pepper, chopped
1/4 cup chopped red onion, sautéed
1/4 cup chopped tomato
1/2 cup chopped cooked ham
1 to 2 cups (4 to 8 ounces) shredded Cheddar cheese
1/2 cup sour cream
1 1/2 teaspoons horseradish

Spread the hash brown potatoes in a lightly buttered 8-inch baking dish. Layer the bell pepper, onion, tomato, ham and cheese in the order listed over the potatoes. Bake at 400 degrees for 15 minutes or until golden brown. Combine the sour cream and horseradish in a bowl and mix well. Serve with the fries. For a larger crowd, double the ingredients and bake in a 9×13-inch baking dish.

*Note:* Use the cubed hash brown potatoes, not the shredded.

*Yield: 4 servings*

*This is a favorite family recipe for special occasions, such as Easter, Thanksgiving, Christmas, and wedding mornings. This recipe works well for such events because it is made the day before and bakes in the oven while your guests are arriving, the children are opening presents, or searching for Easter eggs.*

6 eggs, beaten
2 cups milk
1 (10-ounce) can cream of mushroom soup
10 slices whole wheat bread, cubed
1 to 2 pounds bacon, crisp-cooked, crumbled
12 ounces mild Cheddar cheese, shredded

Combine the eggs, milk and soup in a large bowl and mix well. Add the bread, bacon and cheese and mix well. Pour into a greased baking dish. Refrigerate, covered, overnight. Bake, uncovered, at 250 degrees for 1 1/2 hours.

*Yield: 10 to 12 servings*

# Pigs in Blankets

*This recipe is a Tulip Time tradition from Holland, Michigan.*

2³/₄ to 3 pounds bulk pork sausage
3 cups flour
3 tablespoons baking powder
1 teaspoon salt
1 cup (2 sticks) chilled margarine, cut into pieces
1 cup milk

Divide the sausage by hand or with a fork into 30 to 36 equal portions. Sift the flour, baking powder and salt into a bowl. Cut in the margarine until crumbly. Stir in the milk. Shape the dough into a smooth ball. Roll ¹/₄ inch thick on a floured surface. Cut into 3¹/₂-inch-wide strips. Wrap each sausage portion loosely in a strip of dough. Arrange the sausage rolls seam side down on an ungreased baking sheet. Pierce the top of each sausage roll with a fork. Bake at 400 degrees for 15 minutes. Reduce the oven temperature to 350 degrees. Bake for 15 minutes longer or until brown. You may freeze the baked rolls for up to 4 months.

*Yield: 30 to 36 sausage rolls*

# Mango Salsa

*This salsa makes a flavorful accompaniment to a breakfast buffet; very refreshing for hot summer days.*

¹/₄ cup sugar
¹/₄ cup vinegar
1 bunch green onions (green and white parts), thinly sliced
¹/₄ to ¹/₂ fresh jalapeño chile, seeded, finely chopped
¹/₄ to ¹/₂ cup chopped fresh cilantro
2 large ripe mangoes, chopped

Dissolve the sugar in the vinegar in a small saucepan over low heat, stirring constantly. Pour into a nonreactive serving bowl. Add the green onions, jalapeño chile, cilantro and mangoes and toss gently to coat. Refrigerate, covered, for 1 to 6 hours before serving. This is also excellent served atop grilled fish or chicken.

*Yield: (about) 2 cups*

# Breakfast Pizza

2 (8-count) cans crescent rolls
1 pound bulk pork sausage, cooked, drained
2 cups frozen hash brown potatoes
1 1/2 cups (6 ounces) shredded Cheddar cheese

6 eggs
1/4 cup milk
Salt and pepper to taste
Chopped onion to taste (optional)
Chopped green bell pepper to taste (optional)

Unroll the crescent roll dough and press over the bottom of a 10×15-inch baking pan. Layer evenly with the sausage, potatoes and cheese. Combine the eggs, milk, salt, pepper, onion and bell pepper in a bowl and mix well. Pour over the prepared layers. Top with additional cheese if desired. Bake at 375 degrees for 25 to 35 minutes or until golden brown.

*Yield: 12 servings*

# Wake-Up-Early Casserole

*This recipe was a gift from Mary Early Smith. It makes a fun Christmas Day brunch gift. Wrap the casserole in colorful cellophane and attach the recipe as a gift tag.*

1 (8-count) can crescent rolls
1 pound hot bulk pork sausage
1 cup (4 ounces) shredded Swiss cheese
1 cup milk
1 cup half-and-half

2 tablespoons Dijon mustard
3 or 4 dashes of Tabasco sauce
6 to 8 eggs, beaten
Grated Parmesan cheese to taste
Paprika to taste

Unroll the crescent roll dough and press over the bottom of a 9×13-inch baking dish sprayed with nonstick cooking spray. Cook the sausage in a skillet, stirring until crumbly. Remove with a slotted spoon, allowing some of the drippings to remain on the sausage for flavor. Layer the sausage and Swiss cheese over the dough in the prepared dish. Combine the milk, half-and-half, Dijon mustard, Tabasco sauce and eggs in a bowl and beat with a fork until blended. Pour over the prepared layers. Sprinkle with Parmesan cheese and paprika. You may refrigerate, covered, overnight at this point, or freeze, covered, until ready to use. Thaw completely in the refrigerator before proceeding. Bake at 350 degrees for 50 to 60 minutes or until a fork inserted in the center comes out clean.

*Yield: 10 to 12 servings*

# Shrimp and Grits

*This is great for a buffet table. Use chafing dishes to keep both the shrimp and the grits hot.*

## STONE-GROUND GRITS

2 cups (heaping) stone-ground grits

1/2 cup (1 stick) butter

1 cup half-and-half

1 to 1 1/2 cups heavy cream

2 teaspoons white pepper

## APPLE BACON SHRIMP

8 ounces lean bacon (maple-flavored is recommended)

1 tablespoon butter

1 cup finely chopped onion

1 cup chopped celery

1 cup chopped green bell pepper

1 cup red bell pepper strips

1 tablespoon butter

1/2 cup apple juice

24 ounces deveined peeled fresh shrimp

1 Granny Smith apple, cut into small chunks

*For the grits,* it is important to wash the stone-ground grits 4 or more times as follows: Place the grits in a saucepan and cover with enough water to reach at least 1 1/2 inches above the grits. Bring to a boil over medium-high heat. Drain off water to a level just below the grits as soon as the raw bran begins to float on top. Add enough fresh water to bring the level back to the starting point. Return to a boil and repeat the draining and adding of water at least 3 more times or until there is no longer any bran floating on top.

Cook the grits in enough water to cover in the saucepan, stirring occasionally. Add the butter as soon as the grits begin to thicken. Simmer, covered, for 25 to 30 minutes, adding the half-and-half gradually during the simmering time and stirring to keep the grits from sticking to the pan. Stir in the cream and white pepper just before the end of the cooking time. Add additional butter and milk if the grits are still too coarse. The grits will not be as smooth as quick-cooking grits. Keep the grits warm by placing the entire saucepan inside a second larger pan of simmering water.

*For the shrimp,* fry the bacon in a skillet until crisp. Drain, reserving the drippings. Strain the drippings through a fine sieve, reserving 1 tablespoon and discarding the remainder. Crumble the bacon. Melt 1 tablespoon butter in a large heavy skillet over medium heat. Sauté the onion, celery and bell peppers in the butter for 3 minutes or until the onion is translucent. Add 1 tablespoon butter, the reserved bacon drippings, apple juice and shrimp and stir gently. Cook over medium heat until the shrimp turn pink, adding the apple halfway through the cooking time. Stir in the bacon.

*To serve,* spoon a large portion of the grits onto a serving plate and top with a large helping of the shrimp.

*Yield: 8 to 10 servings*

# Mascarpone Polenta

## MASCARPONE POLENTA

3 cups water
1 1/2 cups cornmeal
1 1/2 cups cold water
1 teaspoon salt

1 1/2 cups (6 ounces) mascarpone
  cheese
Olive oil for brushing

## RED PEPPER SAUCE

2 medium red bell peppers,
  cut into halves
2 teaspoons sugar

2 teaspoons balsamic vinegar
1/8 teaspoon salt

*For the polenta*, bring 3 cups water to a boil in a 3-quart saucepan. Combine the cornmeal, 1 1/2 cups cold water and the salt in a bowl and mix well. Add the cornmeal mixture to the boiling water gradually, stirring constantly. Cook until the mixture returns to a boil, stirring constantly. Reduce the heat to very low. Simmer, covered, for 15 minutes, stirring occasionally. Stir in 1/2 of the cheese. Pour into an ungreased 9×13-inch heatproof pan. Refrigerate, covered, for several hours or until firm.

Cut the polenta into 18 triangles. Arrange on a lightly greased baking sheet and brush the tops with olive oil. Broil 4 to 5 inches from the heat source for 4 minutes. Turn the triangles. Brush with additional olive oil. Spread with the remaining cheese. Broil until the cheese melts.

*For the sauce*, arrange the bell pepper halves cut side down on a foil-lined baking sheet. Bake at 425 degrees for 20 to 25 minutes or until the skins are brown. Place the bell peppers immediately into an unused paper bag. Fold the bag to seal. Let stand until the steam inside the bag loosens the bell pepper skins and the bell peppers are cool enough to handle. Peel and discard the skins using a sharp knife. Combine the bell peppers, sugar, vinegar and salt in a blender and process until smooth. Pour into a small saucepan and heat until the sauce is heated through.

*To serve*, place 2 polenta triangles on each serving plate and spoon some of the sauce over the top.

*Note:* You may substitute any flavorful cheese of choice for the mascarpone cheese.

*Yield: 9 servings*

# Vegetable Cheese Tart

## PARMESAN CRUST
1 stick piecrust mix
1/2 cup grated Parmesan cheese

## VEGETABLE CHEESE FILLING

| | |
|---|---|
| 8 ounces fresh broccoli florets | 1 teaspoon basil |
| 2 cups (8 ounces) shredded Monterey Jack cheese | 1/2 teaspoon thyme |
| 1/2 cup grated Parmesan cheese | 1/4 teaspoon pepper |
| 2 tablespoons flour | 1/4 cup sliced green onions |
| | 2 large tomatoes, sliced, drained |

*For the crust*, prepare the piecrust mix using the package directions and adding the cheese. Roll the dough on a lightly floured surface and fit into a tart pan with a removable bottom. Trim the edge and prick the dough all over with the tines of a fork. Bake at 425 degrees for 10 to 12 minutes. Cool on a wire rack.

*For the filling*, steam the broccoli for 3 minutes or until tender-crisp. Combine the Monterey Jack cheese, Parmesan cheese, flour, basil, thyme, pepper and green onions in a bowl and mix well. Spoon 1/2 of the cheese mixture into the baked tart shell. Layer with the tomatoes and broccoli. Top with the remaining cheese mixture. Bake at 350 degrees for 30 minutes.

*Note:* You may substitute frozen broccoli for the fresh broccoli. Thaw and pat dry before using.

*Yield: 6 to 8 servings*

## Memories

*Early Sandestin owners had to plan their meals more carefully. In the early 1980s, there were few restaurants in the area and even fewer grocery stores available to non-military personnel. Since most meals were prepared at home, many family memories were created in the kitchens of Sandestin.*

# Artichoke Frittata

3 (6-ounce) jars marinated artichokes, drained, finely chopped
1 medium onion, finely chopped
1 garlic clove, finely chopped
4 ounces Gruyère cheese, shredded
4 ounces Parmesan cheese, grated
4 eggs, lightly beaten
6 saltine crackers, finely crushed
Dash of Tabasco sauce
1/2 teaspoon basil

Combine the artichokes, onion, garlic, Gruyère cheese, Parmesan cheese, eggs, cracker crumbs, Tabasco sauce and basil in a large bowl and mix well. Spoon into a buttered 8×8-inch baking pan. Bake at 325 degrees for 1 hour. Cut into 1-inch squares. Serve hot or at room temperature.

*Yield: 64 squares*

# John Wayne Eggs

16 ounces Cheddar cheese, shredded
16 ounces Monterey Jack cheese, shredded
2 (4-ounce) cans whole green chiles, seeded, chopped
4 egg yolks
2 tablespoons flour
Salt and pepper to taste
1 (5-ounce) can evaporated milk
4 egg whites, stiffly beaten
Sliced fresh tomatoes to taste

Combine the Cheddar cheese, Monterey Jack cheese and green chiles in a bowl and toss to mix. Spoon into a buttered baking dish. Combine the egg yolks, flour, salt, pepper and evaporated milk in a bowl and mix well. Fold in the egg whites. Pour over the cheese mixture in the prepared dish. Bake at 300 degrees for 30 minutes. Top with the tomatoes and serve.

*Yield: 6 to 8 servings*

# The Floridian Crabmeat Omelette

**FLORIDIAN BUTTER**

2 cups (4 sticks) butter, softened

4 ounces fresh parsley, stems
removed, finely chopped

1/2 cup white wine, such as
chardonnay or pinot blanc

2 ounces garlic powder

**CRABMEAT OMELETTE**

1/2 cup Floridian Butter

3 ounces lump crabmeat, shells
removed and flaked

3 eggs, well beaten

2 ounces cream cheese, cut into strips

1/2 cup (2 ounces) shredded Monterey
Jack cheese

*For the butter,* beat the butter in a mixing bowl for 8 minutes or until fluffy. Add the parsley, wine and garlic powder and mix at low speed until well blended. Refrigerate, covered, until ready to use.

*For the omelette,* melt the Floridian Butter in a small saucepan over low heat. Add the crabmeat and cook for 1 minute, stirring occasionally. Set aside. Butter or spray an omelette pan with nonstick cooking spray. Heat the pan over medium heat. Pour in the eggs. Arrange the cream cheese strips over the eggs just as the eggs begin to set. Flip the omelette upside down and count to 15. Flip the omelette back to the original position. This process will melt the cream cheese into the omelette.

Fold the omelette in half and slide onto an ovenproof ceramic serving plate. Pour the crabmeat mixture over the omelette and sprinkle with the Monterey Jack cheese. Place in a warm oven and heat until the cheese melts. Serve with an English muffin and hash brown potatoes. Garnish with fruit.

*Yield: 1 or 2 servings*

*Another Broken Egg Café*

# Country Ham

Center cut country ham slices
Vegetable oil
Brewed coffee

Cut each ham slice into 6 equal pieces. Brown the ham in hot oil in a skillet. Drain on paper towels, discarding some of the oil in the pan. Add equal amounts of water and coffee to the skillet. Return the ham to the skillet. Simmer for 1 hour or until the ham is fork-tender. For a party, serve small pieces of the country ham on a roll or biscuit.

*Yield: variable*


# Baked Orange Cups

6 medium oranges
6 medium apples, peeled, chopped
1 (8-ounce) can crushed pineapple
1 cup sugar
Butter
1/2 cup chopped pecans

Cut each orange into halves, carving a decorative zigzag edge. Remove the centers, discarding the seeds and membranes and leaving a thin shell of orange inside the peels. Stand the orange cups in a shallow baking dish. Combine the orange centers, apples, undrained pineapple and sugar in a saucepan and mix well. Cook until very thick, stirring frequently. Divide the mixture evenly among the orange cups. Dot with butter and sprinkle with the pecans. Pour a small amount of water into the dish. Bake at 325 degrees for 30 minutes.

*Yield: 12 servings*

# Curried Fruit

1 (29-ounce) can pear halves

1 (29-ounce) can freestone peach halves

1 (17-ounce) can pitted Royal Anne light sweet cherries

1 (20-ounce) can pineapple chunks

1 (11-ounce) can mandarin oranges

1 (17-ounce) can peeled apricots

1/2 cup golden raisins

3/4 cup sugar

1/4 teaspoon salt

3 tablespoons butter, softened

3 tablespoons flour

1/2 to 1 teaspoon curry powder

1/2 cup white wine

Drain the pears, peaches, cherries, pineapple, oranges and apricots, reserving the juice in a bowl. Stir the reserved juices to mix. Reserve 3/4 cup of the mixed juices, discarding the remainder. Soak the raisins in hot water to cover in a bowl for 10 minutes; drain. Combine the reserved juice, sugar, salt, butter and flour in a small saucepan and mix well. Cook the mixture over medium heat until thickened, stirring constantly; do not boil. Combine the fruit in a large bowl and mix gently. Fold in the butter mixture. Add the curry powder and wine and stir to mix. Let stand for 3 hours. Spoon into a baking dish. Bake at 350 degrees for 30 minutes. Serve immediately or refrigerate, covered, overnight and reheat the next day. The flavor improves with age.

*Yield: 8 to 10 servings*

# Lunch on the Deck

# Grape Salad

8 ounces cream cheese, softened
1 cup sour cream
1/2 cup sugar
1 teaspoon vanilla extract
4 cups green seedless grapes, patted dry
4 cups red seedless grapes, patted dry
1/2 cup packed light brown sugar
1/2 cup chopped pecans

Combine the cream cheese, sour cream, sugar and vanilla in a bowl and mix well. Fold in the grapes. Combine the brown sugar and pecans in a bowl and toss to mix. Add 1/2 of the pecan mixture to the grape mixture and mix well. Spoon into a serving bowl. Sprinkle with the remaining pecan mixture. Refrigerate, covered, for several hours before serving. Leftovers will freeze well.

*Yield: 6 to 8 servings*

# Frozen Fruit Salad

2 cups sour cream
2 tablespoons lemon juice
1/2 cup sugar
1/8 teaspoon salt
4 drops of red food coloring
1 banana, chopped
1/4 cup chopped pecans
1 (8-ounce) can crushed pineapple, drained
1 (17-ounce) can fruit cocktail, drained

Combine the sour cream, lemon juice, sugar, salt and food coloring in a bowl and mix well. Fold in the banana, pecans, pineapple and fruit cocktail. Divide the mixture evenly among 12 paper-lined muffin cups. Freeze, covered with plastic wrap, until firm.

*Note:* For Sandestin Popsicles, insert a popsicle stick into the center of each filled muffin cup before freezing.

*Yield: 12 servings*

# Apricot Salad

1 (6-ounce) package or 2 (3-ounce) packages apricot gelatin
1 (15-ounce) can crushed pineapple
2 cups buttermilk
8 ounces frozen whipped topping, thawed
1/2 cup chopped pecans (optional)

Combine the gelatin and undrained pineapple in a saucepan and mix well. Bring to a boil, stirring constantly. Remove from the heat. Let stand until cool. Stir in the buttermilk. Fold in the whipped topping and pecans. Pour into a serving dish and garnish with additional pecans. Refrigerate, covered, until serving time.

*Yield: 6 servings*

# Peach Surprise

1 (16-ounce) can peaches
1/2 cup sugar
1 teaspoon nutmeg
1 (3-ounce) package lemon gelatin

Drain the peaches, reserving the liquid. Purée the peaches in a blender; set aside. Add enough water to the reserved liquid to measure 1 cup. Pour the mixture into a saucepan. Add the sugar and nutmeg and mix well. Bring to a boil, stirring constantly. Boil for 1 minute, stirring constantly. Place the gelatin in a heatproof bowl. Stir in the boiling sugar mixture. Stir until the gelatin is dissolved. Add the puréed peaches and mix well. Pour into a gelatin mold sprayed with nonstick cooking spray. Refrigerate, covered, overnight or until set. Unmold onto a serving plate.

*Yield: 8 servings*

# Tomato Aspic

1 envelope unflavored gelatin
2 cups vegetable juice cocktail
1/8 teaspoon Tabasco sauce, or to taste
1 teaspoon lemon juice

Soften the gelatin in 1/2 cup of the vegetable juice cocktail in a bowl, stirring to mix. Heat the remaining vegetable juice cocktail in a saucepan. Stir in the Tabasco sauce and lemon juice. Add the gelatin mixture, stirring until the gelatin is completely dissolved. Taste the mixture and correct the seasonings if necessary. Pour into individual gelatin molds sprayed with nonstick cooking spray. Refrigerate, covered, for several hours or until set. Unmold onto individual serving plates.

*Yield: 5 or 6 servings*

# Congealed Spinach Salad

1 (10-ounce) package frozen spinach, thawed
1 (6-ounce) package lemon gelatin
2 cups boiling water
12 ounces small curd cottage cheese
1/3 cup vinegar
1 cup finely chopped celery
1/2 cup chopped green onions
1/2 cup finely chopped red bell pepper
1 cup mayonnaise (no substitutions)

Drain the spinach, pressing out the excess moisture. Dissolve the gelatin in the boiling water in a heatproof bowl, stirring to mix. Let stand until cool. Add the spinach, cottage cheese, vinegar, celery, green onions and bell pepper and mix well. Fold in the mayonnaise. Pour into a gelatin mold sprayed with nonstick cooking spray. Refrigerate, covered, until firm. Unmold onto a serving plate.

*Yield: 6 to 8 servings*

# Three-Bean Salad

1 (16-ounce) can green beans, drained
1 (16-ounce) can garbanzo beans, drained
1 (16-ounce) can kidney beans, rinsed, drained
1 (16-ounce) can yellow wax beans, drained
1 green bell pepper, chopped
2 medium onions, chopped
2 cups chopped celery
1/2 cup chopped fresh parsley
1/2 cup vegetable oil
1/4 cup red wine vinegar or cider vinegar
2 tablespoons sugar
2 teaspoons salt

Combine the green beans, garbanzo beans, kidney beans, yellow wax beans, bell pepper, onions, celery and parsley in a large bowl and toss to mix. Combine the oil, vinegar, sugar and salt in a small bowl and whisk to blend. Pour over the bean mixture and toss to coat. Refrigerate, covered, for several hours to allow the flavors to blend.

*Yield: 10 servings*

# Corn Salad

2 cups cooked corn kernels
1 medium tomato, seeded, chopped
1 rib celery, chopped
1/4 cup sliced green onions
1 tablespoon minced fresh parsley

1/4 cup mayonnaise
1 tablespoon vinegar
3/4 teaspoon salt
1/2 teaspoon sugar
1/8 teaspoon pepper

Combine the corn, tomato, celery, green onions and parsley in a large bowl and toss to mix. Combine the mayonnaise, vinegar, salt, sugar and pepper in a small bowl and whisk to blend. Pour over the salad and toss to coat. Spoon into a serving bowl. Refrigerate, covered, until ready to serve.

*Yield: 4 servings*

# Spinach, Avocado and Strawberry Salad

*This is an especially pretty salad at Christmas.*

## POPPY SEED DRESSING

1 cup vegetable oil
1/2 cup sugar
1/3 cup cider vinegar
1 tablespoon poppy seeds

1 teaspoon salt
1 teaspoon dry mustard
1/4 teaspoon paprika

## SPINACH AND AVOCADO SALAD

1 pound fresh spinach
1 purple onion, sliced

1 avocado, sliced lengthwise
1 pint strawberries, cut into quarters

*For the dressing,* combine the oil, sugar, vinegar, poppy seeds, salt, dry mustard and paprika in a bowl and whisk to blend. Refrigerate, covered, until ready to use. Stir before using. Use within 1 week.

*For the salad,* layer the spinach, onion, avocado and strawberries on a salad plate. Pour the dressing over the salad and serve.

*Yield: 6 to 8 servings*

# Broccoli Salad

1 large bunch broccoli, chopped
1/2 medium red onion, chopped
1 cup red seedless grapes
3 ounces sunflower seeds
1 cup raisins

10 slices bacon, crisp-cooked,
  crumbled
1/2 cup mayonnaise
1/4 cup sugar
1 tablespoon red wine vinegar

Combine the broccoli, onion, grapes, sunflower seeds, raisins and bacon in a large bowl and toss to mix. Combine the mayonnaise, sugar and vinegar in a small bowl and whisk to blend. Pour over the salad and toss to coat. Spoon into a serving bowl. Refrigerate, covered, overnight.

*Yield: 4 to 6 servings*

# Marinated Vegetable Salad

1 envelope ranch salad dressing mix
3/4 cup vegetable oil
1/4 cup red wine vinegar
1 (20-ounce) package frozen California blend vegetables
3 ribs celery, sliced
1/2 cup sliced green olives
1 small can pitted black olives, drained
1 (8-ounce) jar sliced mushrooms, drained
1 medium onion, sliced, separated into rings
1 1/2 cups grape or cherry tomatoes, cut into halves

Combine the salad dressing mix, oil and vinegar in a small bowl and whisk to blend; set aside. Microwave the frozen vegetables in a large microwave-safe container for 2 to 3 minutes; drain well. Add the celery, green olives, black olives, mushrooms, onion and tomatoes and mix gently. Pour the dressing over the salad and mix gently to coat. Spoon into a glass serving dish. Refrigerate, covered, for 24 hours, stirring the mixture 2 or 3 times. Leftovers may be stored in the refrigerator for several days.

*Note:* You may drain the mixture after marinating and arrange it on a platter with wooden picks for a quick pick-up appetizer.

*Yield: 6 to 8 servings*

# Baby Spinach Salad

## WARM BACON DRESSING

4 ounces applewood smoked bacon
1/2 cup red wine vinegar
1/4 cup packed brown sugar

1 cup honey mustard
Dash of Worcestershire sauce
Dash of Tabasco sauce

## SPINACH SALAD

1 package baby spinach
1 cup button mushrooms, sliced

4 hard-cooked eggs, chopped
Fresh cracked pepper to taste

**For the dressing,** cook the bacon in a skillet until crisp. Drain on paper towels, reserving the drippings in the pan. Crumble the bacon. Stir the vinegar and brown sugar into the bacon drippings. Increase the heat, stirring constantly. Stir in the honey mustard, Worcestershire sauce and Tabasco sauce. Keep warm over low heat, stirring occasionally.

**For the salad,** arrange the spinach on a serving plate. Spoon the mushrooms, bacon and eggs across the salad in a row. Toss the salad at the table with the warm dressing. Sprinkle with pepper.

*Yield: 4 servings*

*Seagar's Prime Steaks & Seafood*

# Baby Bleu Salad

### BALSAMIC VINAIGRETTE

1/2 cup balsamic vinegar

3 tablespoons Dijon mustard

3 tablespoons honey

2 garlic cloves, minced

2 small shallots, minced

1/4 teaspoon salt

1/4 teaspoon pepper

1 cup olive oil

### SWEET-AND-SPICY PECANS

1/4 cup sugar

1 cup warm water

1 cup pecan halves

2 tablespoons sugar

1 tablespoon chili powder

1/8 teaspoon ground red pepper
   (cayenne)

### BABY BLEU SALAD

12 ounces mixed salad greens

4 ounces bleu cheese, crumbled

2 oranges, peeled, thinly sliced

1 pint fresh strawberries,
   cut into quarters

*For the vinaigrette,* combine the vinegar, Dijon mustard, honey, garlic, shallots, salt and pepper in a bowl and whisk to blend. Add the olive oil in a fine stream, whisking constantly until blended.

*For the pecans,* combine 1/4 cup sugar and the water in a bowl and stir until the sugar dissolves. Add the pecans and let stand for 10 minutes. Drain the pecans, discarding the liquid. Combine 2 tablespoons sugar, the chili powder and red pepper in a bowl and mix well. Add the pecans, tossing to coat. Spread the pecans on a lightly greased baking sheet. Bake at 350 degrees for 10 minutes, stirring once.

*For the salad,* toss the salad greens with the vinaigrette and the bleu cheese in a salad bowl or on a serving platter. Arrange the orange slices over the top. Sprinkle with the strawberries and top with the pecans.

*Yield: 6 servings*

## ITALIAN GARLIC DRESSING

1¹/2 tablespoons fresh lemon juice

1 tablespoon white wine vinegar

1 tablespoon Worcestershire sauce

Dash of Tabasco sauce

1 teaspoon dry mustard

1 teaspoon sugar

1 teaspoon Italian seasoning

Salt and freshly ground pepper
 to taste

2 (or more) large garlic cloves

5 tablespoons olive oil

## ROMAINE SALAD

1 head romaine, torn

2 tablespoons grated Parmesan cheese

¹/2 cup croutons

*For the dressing,* combine the lemon juice, vinegar, Worcestershire sauce, Tabasco sauce, dry mustard, sugar, Italian seasoning, salt, pepper and garlic in a blender and process until smooth. Add the olive oil in a fine stream, processing constantly until well blended.

*For the salad,* place the romaine in a salad bowl. Pour the dressing over the romaine. Top with the cheese and croutons and toss gently. Serve with a quality white wine and cold chicken or smoked fish.

*Yield: 4 to 6 servings*

*Memories*

*Annalee and Brian Flanagan came to Sandestin in 1992 and fell in love with the Olde Town area. They remember fondly visiting with her mom, two sisters, and three-year-old niece, Kaitlin. Kaitlin loved the beach. In fact, she loved it so much that they had to restrain her until the car was parked, because she would try to get out of the car as soon as they turned into the parking lot. As soon as the door opened, she was out like a shot, running to the beach, with the rest of them running to keep up with her.*

# Red Cabbage, Bay Shrimp and Tangerine Salad

### TANGERINE SALAD DRESSING

1 small can tangerine sections

2 tablespoons white wine vinegar

1 tablespoon balsamic vinegar

1 tablespoon light soy sauce

1/2 teaspoon honey

1/2 teaspoon curry powder

1/8 teaspoon cayenne pepper

2 teaspoons minced fresh gingerroot

Grated Parmesan cheese to taste
  (optional)

6 tablespoons extra-virgin olive oil

### CABBAGE AND SHRIMP SALAD

1 head red cabbage, cut into halves,
  finely shredded

Dash of salt

1 pound deveined peeled fresh Bay
  shrimp, rinsed

2 tablespoons chopped green onions

*For the dressing*, drain the tangerine sections, reserving the liquid. Combine the white wine vinegar, balsamic vinegar, soy sauce, honey, curry powder, cayenne pepper, gingerroot, cheese and reserved tangerine liquid in a glass bowl and whisk until blended. Add the olive oil in a fine stream, whisking constantly until blended. Whisk vigorously just before using.

*For the salad*, rinse the cabbage with cold water; drain. Dry thoroughly with paper towels. Sprinkle with the salt. Heat a wok or sauté pan over high heat until very hot. Add 3 tablespoons of the dressing carefully to the wok. Stir-fry the cabbage, in batches, for 30 to 40 seconds each. Remove to a warm plate using a slotted spoon. The cabbage should still be crunchy. Add additional dressing to the wok if necessary. Add the shrimp and stir-fry until the shrimp turn pink. Reserve 4 or 5 tangerine sections. Add the remaining tangerine sections to the wok and stir-fry for a few seconds. Remove the shrimp and tangerine sections to the plate with the cabbage. If too much liquid remains in the wok, reduce the liquid by 1/2 over high heat. Toss the shrimp, tangerines and cabbage in a salad bowl. Drizzle with the reduced dressing. Sprinkle with the green onions and reserved tangerine sections and serve.

*Yield: 6 to 8 servings*

## Coleslaw

CIDER VINEGAR DRESSING

1 cup canola oil

2 tablespoons cider vinegar

1/4 cup sugar

Flavor packet from chicken ramen
 noodles (below)

COLESLAW

1 (3-ounce) package chicken ramen
 noodles

1 large package coleslaw mix

1/2 cup sunflower seeds

1 cup roasted almond slivers

1/2 bunch green onions, chopped

*For the dressing,* combine the canola oil, vinegar, sugar and the flavor packet from the ramen noodles in a bowl and whisk to blend. Refrigerate, covered, for 2 hours or longer before using.

*For the coleslaw,* break the ramen noodles. Combine the ramen noodles, coleslaw mix, sunflower seeds, almonds and green onions in a bowl and toss to mix. Pour 1/2 of the dressing over the coleslaw and toss to mix. Serve immediately. Reserve the remaining dressing for another batch of coleslaw or other use.

*Yield: 6 to 8 servings*

# Bok Choy Salad

**SESAME NOODLES**

1/4 cup (1/2 stick) butter or margarine

3 tablespoons sugar

2 (3-ounce) packages ramen noodles

3/4 cup sliced almonds

1/4 cup sesame seeds

**GARLIC SOY SALAD DRESSING**

3/4 cup sugar

1/2 cup red wine vinegar

1/4 cup soy sauce

1 teaspoon minced garlic

3/4 cup vegetable oil

**BOK CHOY SALAD**

1 bunch bok choy (green part and stems), cut into 1-inch pieces

1/2 cup sliced green onions

*For the noodles,* melt the butter with the sugar in a heavy skillet over medium heat, stirring to combine. Reserve the flavor packets from the ramen noodles for another use. Break the noodles into small pieces. Sauté the noodles, almonds and sesame seeds in the butter mixture until golden brown, stirring frequently. Remove to a plate to cool. Crush the mixture slightly.

*For the salad dressing,* combine the sugar, vinegar, soy sauce and garlic in a bowl and whisk to blend. Add the oil in a fine stream, whisking constantly until blended.

*For the salad,* combine the bok choy and green onions in a salad bowl and toss to mix. Sprinkle with the desired amount of noodle mixture and toss to mix. Pour about 1/2 of the dressing over the salad and toss gently to coat. Reserve the remaining dressing for another use.

*Note:* You may freeze any leftover noodle mixture in a sealable plastic freezer bag.

*Yield: 6 to 8 servings*

# Raspberry Vinaigrette

1 1/2 cups raspberry wine vinegar
Juice of 1 lemon
1 teaspoon Dijon mustard
1 teaspoon basil
Sugar to taste
1/2 cup olive oil
1/2 cup vegetable oil
Salt and pepper to taste

Combine the vinegar, lemon juice, Dijon mustard, basil and sugar in a bowl and whisk to blend. Add the olive oil in a fine stream, whisking constantly until blended. Add the vegetable oil in a fine stream, whisking constantly until blended. Season with salt and pepper.

*Yield: (about) 3 cups*

# Tomato Vinaigrette

1 (10-ounce) can tomato soup
3/4 cup vinegar
1 onion, grated
2 tablespoons Worcestershire sauce
1/2 cup sugar
2 teaspoons dry mustard
2 teaspoons salt
1/2 teaspoon pepper
1 cup vegetable oil
2 garlic cloves, peeled

Combine the soup, vinegar, onion, Worcestershire sauce, sugar, mustard, salt and pepper in a blender and process until smooth. Add the oil in a fine stream, processing until blended. Add the whole garlic cloves and stir. Refrigerate, covered, until ready to use. Remove the garlic cloves before serving.

*Yield: (about) 3 1/2 cups*

# Bleu Cheese Dressing

3/4 cup sour cream

1/2 teaspoon dry mustard

1/2 teaspoon salt

1/2 teaspoon pepper

1/3 teaspoon garlic powder

1 teaspoon Worcestershire sauce

1 1/3 cups mayonnaise

4 ounces bleu cheese

Combine the sour cream, dry mustard, salt, pepper, garlic powder and Worcestershire sauce in a blender. Blend at low speed for 2 minutes. Add the mayonnaise and blend at low speed for 30 seconds. Blend at medium speed for 2 minutes. Crumble the bleu cheese into very small pieces and add to the mixture. Blend at low speed for 4 minutes.

*Yield: (about) 2 1/2 cups*

# Ranch Dressing

15 (2-inch-square) saltine crackers

1 cup parsley flakes

1/2 cup dried minced onion

2 tablespoons dill weed

1/2 cup onion salt

1/2 cup garlic salt

1/4 cup onion powder

1/4 cup garlic powder

1 cup mayonnaise

1 cup buttermilk

Process the crackers in a food processor at high speed until of a powder consistency. Add the parsley flakes, onion, dill weed, onion salt, garlic salt, onion powder and garlic powder and process to a fine powder. Store in an airtight container at room temperature, out of direct sunlight and away from heat or moisture, for up to 1 year. To use, combine 1 tablespoon of the herb mixture with the mayonnaise and buttermilk in a bowl and mix well.

*Yield: 2 cups dressing*

# Curried Rice Artichoke Salad

4 cups water
2 chicken bouillon cubes
2 cups uncooked rice
2 tablespoons butter
1 garlic clove, minced
1 cup vermicelli, broken into
   1/4- to 1/2-inch pieces
2 (6-ounce) jars marinated artichokes,
   drained

5 green onions, chopped
1 green bell pepper, chopped
1/2 cup black olives, sliced
1 (4-ounce) jar chopped pimentos,
   drained
3 ribs celery, chopped
2 cups mayonnaise (no substitutions)
1 tablespoon curry powder
2 teaspoons seasoned salt

Bring the water to a boil in a saucepan. Dissolve the bouillon cubes in the boiling water. Add the rice and stir to mix. Cook the rice using the package directions; set aside. Melt the butter in a skillet over medium heat. Add the garlic and pasta and cook until the pasta is brown, stirring frequently. Stir the pasta mixture into the rice mixture. Add the artichokes, green onions, bell pepper, olives, pimentos and celery and mix well. Combine the mayonnaise, curry powder and seasoned salt in a bowl and mix well. Fold into the rice mixture. Spoon into a serving bowl. Refrigerate, covered, overnight. Serve cold or at room temperature.

*Yield: 8 to 10 servings*

# Cold Wild Rice Salad

3 cups cooked wild rice
3 cups chopped cooked chicken
1 cup water chestnuts, chopped
1/2 cup finely chopped celery
1/2 cup finely chopped onion
2 cups mayonnaise-type salad
   dressing

1/4 teaspoon curry powder (optional)
1 teaspoon seasoned salt
1 teaspoon soy sauce
Dash of dill weed
1 cup cashews
2 cups red seedless grapes

Combine the wild rice, chicken, water chestnuts, celery and onion in a bowl and mix well. Combine the salad dressing, curry powder, seasoned salt, soy sauce and dill weed in a bowl and whisk to blend. Spoon over the chicken mixture and mix gently but thoroughly. Fold in the cashews and grapes just before serving.

*Yield: 8 to 10 servings*

# Orzo Salad with Feta, Olives and Peppers

## LEMON GARLIC DRESSING

3 tablespoons fresh lemon juice

1 tablespoon white wine vinegar

1 tablespoon minced garlic

1½ teaspoons oregano

1 teaspoon Dijon mustard

1 teaspoon cumin

½ cup olive oil

Salt and pepper to taste

## ORZO AND FETA SALAD

12 ounces orzo (rice-shaped pasta)

Salt to taste

2 tablespoons olive oil

1½ cups (6 ounces) crumbled
seasoned feta cheese

1 cup chopped red bell pepper

1 cup chopped yellow bell pepper

¾ cup pitted kalamata olives

4 green onions, chopped

2 tablespoons drained capers

Pepper to taste

3 tablespoons pine nuts, toasted

*For the dressing,* combine the lemon juice, vinegar, garlic, oregano, Dijon mustard and cumin in a small bowl and whisk to blend. Add the olive oil in a fine stream, whisking constantly until blended. Season with salt and pepper.

*For the salad,* cook the pasta in a large pot of boiling salted water until tender but still firm, or al dente; drain. Rinse with cold water; drain well. Toss the pasta with the olive oil in a large bowl. Add the cheese, bell peppers, olives, green onions and capers and mix well. Pour the dressing over the pasta mixture and toss to coat. Season with salt and pepper. Sprinkle with the pine nuts and serve. You may prepare the salad up to 6 hours ahead. Refrigerate, covered, until serving time.

*Yield: 8 to 10 servings*

## Local Interest

*The local Choctawhatchee Audubon Society sponsors a variety of bird-related activities in Walton and Okaloosa counties. Beginner's Bird Walks are held at least once monthly on Saturday mornings, at no cost. It is a good way to see more of the area and learn some helpful birding tips from people in the know. The golf courses, marina, beach, tennis courts, and walking path all have varied habitats that are home to some kind of feathered creatures—be they locals, or those just stopping by for a brief visit.*

# Vegetable Pasta Salad

*Make-ahead dishes help everyone enjoy a vacation. This refrigerated pasta salad makes a great accompaniment to sandwiches or grilled meats and keeps for several days.*

## MUSTARD VINAIGRETTE

1/2 teaspoon dry mustard or Dijon
    mustard
Pinch of sugar

1/3 cup canola oil
1/3 cup vinegar

## VEGETABLE PASTA SALAD

Vegetable oil
16 ounces farfalle, shells or fusilli,
    cooked al dente, drained
1 cucumber, peeled, seeded,
    chopped
1/3 small Vidalia onion, chopped
2 ribs celery, chopped
2 carrots, peeled, sliced

1 cup broccoli florets, chopped
1 small can sliced black olives, drained
1 (6-ounce) jar marinated artichoke
    hearts, drained, coarsely chopped
1 pint cherry tomatoes, cut into halves
1 tablespoon chopped fresh parsley
Salt and pepper to taste

*For the dressing,* combine the dry mustard, sugar, oil and vinegar in a small bowl and whisk to blend.

*For the salad,* add a small amount of vegetable oil to the drained pasta in a large bowl, stirring to keep the pasta from sticking together. Refrigerate, covered, while preparing the salad. Combine the cucumber, onion, celery, carrots, broccoli, olives, artichokes, tomatoes, parsley, salt and pepper in a large bowl and toss to mix.

Add the dressing and pasta to the vegetable mixture and mix well. Refrigerate, covered, for several hours, stirring occasionally. Taste and adjust the seasonings. Prepare and add additional dressing if the pasta seems dry. You may substitute a bottled vinaigrette for the homemade dressing.

*Note:* For a main dish salad, add shredded Cheddar cheese and chopped cooked ham, or bell pepper and pepperoni slices.

*Yield: 10 to 12 servings*

## Spaghetti Salad

**MARINATED SPAGHETTI**

16 ounces spaghetti, broken into
   halves
2 tablespoons Lawry's seasoned salt

Coarsely ground pepper to taste
3 tablespoons lemon juice
1/4 cup vegetable oil

**SHRIMP AND VEGETABLE SALAD**

2 cups chopped celery
1 cup chopped green bell pepper
1 medium onion, chopped
1 can sliced black olives, drained

1 (2-ounce) jar sliced pimento, drained
1 pound peeled cooked shrimp
1 1/2 cups (about) mayonnaise

*For the spaghetti,* cook the pasta using the package directions; drain. Combine the pasta, seasoned salt, pepper, lemon juice and oil in a bowl and mix well. Marinate, covered, overnight.

*For the salad,* combine the celery, bell pepper, onion, olives, pimento, shrimp and mayonnaise in a large bowl and mix well. Add the marinated spaghetti to the shrimp mixture and mix well. You may substitute ham and cheese for the shrimp.

*Yield: 10 to 12 servings*

## Chicken Salad

3 or 4 boneless skinless chicken breasts
1 (8-ounce) bottle Italian salad
   dressing
Butter for toasting
Chopped pecans or almonds to taste
1 (8-ounce) can crushed pineapple,
   drained

3 ribs celery, chopped
1 sweet onion, chopped
1/4 cup mayonnaise
Old Bay seasoning to taste

Arrange the chicken in a shallow nonreactive dish. Pour the salad dressing over the chicken. Refrigerate, covered, for several hours, turning occasionally. Drain the chicken, discarding the marinade. Grill the chicken on a grill rack over hot coals until cooked through, turning once. Cool slightly and cut into bite-size pieces. Melt a small amount of butter in a skillet over medium heat. Sauté the pecans in the butter until toasted, stirring constantly; cool. Combine the chicken, pecans, pineapple, celery, onion, mayonnaise and Old Bay seasoning in a bowl and mix well. Refrigerate, covered, until serving time.

*Yield: 4 to 6 servings*

# Teddy's Shrimp Salad

8 ounces peeled steamed shrimp, chilled
2 hard-cooked eggs, chopped
1 large rib celery, chopped
1 tablespoon chopped onion
Low-fat mayonnaise to taste
Salt and white pepper to taste

Reserve 3 or 4 of the shrimp. Chop the remaining shrimp finely. Combine the chopped shrimp, eggs, celery, onion and enough mayonnaise to hold the mixture together in a bowl and mix well. Season with salt and white pepper. Spoon into a serving bowl. Top with the reserved whole shrimp. Refrigerate, covered, until serving time.

*Yield: 4 servings*

# Corn Bread Salad

1 (8-ounce) package corn muffin mix
1 (4-ounce) can chopped green chiles
1/8 teaspoon cumin
1/8 teaspoon oregano
Pinch of rubbed sage
1 cup mayonnaise
1 cup sour cream
1 envelope ranch salad dressing mix
2 (15-ounce) cans pinto beans, rinsed,
  drained

2 (15-ounce) cans whole kernel corn,
  drained
3 medium tomatoes, chopped
1 cup chopped green bell pepper
1 cup chopped green onions
10 slices bacon, crisp-cooked,
  crumbled
2 cups (8 ounces) shredded Cheddar
  cheese

Prepare the corn muffin batter using the package directions. Stir in the undrained green chiles, cumin, oregano and sage. Spread in a greased 8×8-inch baking pan. Bake at 400 degrees for 20 to 25 minutes or until a wooden pick inserted in the center comes out clean. Cool in the pan on a wire rack. Combine the mayonnaise, sour cream and salad dressing mix in a bowl and whisk to blend. Crumble the corn bread. Layer the corn bread, beans, mayonnaise mixture, corn, tomatoes, bell pepper, green onions, bacon and cheese 1/2 at a time in a 9×13-inch dish. The dish will be very full. Refrigerate, covered, for 2 hours.

*Yield: 12 servings*

# Sweet Sandwiches

3 egg yolks
1/2 cup (1 stick) butter
1 cup sugar
1 cup raisins
1 cup chopped pecans

1 (8-ounce) can crushed pineapple,
  drained
Mayonnaise to taste
Sliced white sandwich bread

Combine the egg yolks, butter and sugar in the top of a double boiler over simmering water. Cook until the butter melts and the mixture thickens, stirring constantly. Remove from the heat. Stir in the raisins, pecans and pineapple. Spread mayonnaise over bread slices and top with the pineapple mixture to make sandwiches.

*Yield: variable*

# Olive Nut Spread

1 (8-ounce) jar salad olives
6 ounces cream cheese, softened

1/2 cup mayonnaise
1 cup chopped pecans

Drain the olives, reserving 2 tablespoons of the liquid. Chop enough of the olives to measure 1 cup. Reserve any remaining olives for another use. Combine the cream cheese and mayonnaise in a bowl and mix well. Add the chopped olives, reserved olive liquid and pecans and mix well. Refrigerate, covered, overnight. Serve as a filling for sandwiches.

*Yield: (about) 3 1/2 cups spread*

# Chicken Chutney Spread

1 pound chopped cooked chicken
8 ounces cream cheese, softened
1/4 cup mayonnaise
1/3 cup finely chopped green onions

2 tablespoons chutney
1 teaspoon curry powder
Dash of pepper
1/4 cup slivered almonds, toasted

Process the chicken in a food processor fitted with the steel blade for 5 seconds. Add the cream cheese, mayonnaise, green onions, chutney, curry powder and pepper and process for 5 to 10 seconds or until well blended. Spoon into an au gratin baking dish. Sprinkle with the almonds. Bake at 300 degrees for 20 to 30 minutes or until light brown. Serve as a sandwich filling or with crackers and chips.

*Yield: 4 to 5 cups spread*

# Ham and Cheese Roll-Ups

1 (8-count) can crescent rolls
4 slices deli ham
4 teaspoons prepared mustard

1 cup (4 ounces) shredded Swiss
  cheese

Unroll the crescent roll dough and separate into 4 long rectangles. Press the perforations to seal. Place 1 ham slice over each rectangle. Spread each with 1 teaspoon prepared mustard. Sprinkle each with 1/4 cup of the cheese. Roll each rectangle as for a jelly roll, starting at the longest side. Cut into 1/2-inch slices. Arrange on an ungreased baking sheet. Bake at 375 degrees for 15 to 20 minutes or until light brown.

*Yield: variable*

# Stuffed Sandwich Loaf

*This is excellent for an island picnic. Place the wrapped stuffed loaf in the refrigerator the night before the picnic. Pack the sandwich the next morning and cut it into serving wedges on-site.*

1 (1-pound) round loaf sourdough
    bread
3 tablespoons low-fat mayonnaise
2 teaspoons lime juice
1/2 teaspoon cumin
4 ounces thinly sliced smoked turkey
    breast, cut into 1/2-inch strips
12 thin slices tomato

1/2 cup julienned red bell pepper
1/2 cup (2 ounces) shredded low-
    sodium Swiss cheese
3/4 cup alfalfa sprouts
1 1/4 cups shredded iceberg lettuce
1/3 cup salsa
1 tablespoon chopped fresh cilantro

Slice off the top 1/3 of the bread loaf using a large serrated knife. Remove the centers from the top and bottom portions, leaving a 1/2-inch-thick shell. Reserve the removed bread centers for another use. Combine the mayonnaise, lime juice and cumin in a bowl and mix well. Spread the mixture evenly in the hollow bread shells. Layer the bottom portion with the turkey, tomato, bell pepper, cheese, alfalfa sprouts, lettuce, salsa and cilantro 1/2 at a time, pressing down firmly after the first layer of ingredients. Cover with the top bread portion and press down firmly. Wrap the stuffed loaf tightly with heavy-duty plastic wrap. Refrigerate for 4 hours or longer. To serve, remove the plastic wrap and cut the loaf into wedges.

*Yield: 6 servings*

# Homemade Focaccia

2¼ teaspoons dry yeast
1½ cups warm water
¼ cup olive oil
24 ounces bread flour
2 tablespoons sugar
¾ teaspoon salt
¼ cup olives, chopped
¼ cup chopped red bell pepper

2 tablespoons chopped garlic
Chopped fresh rosemary, oregano,
  basil or thyme to taste
Crushed dried red chiles to taste
Sautéed vegetables to taste
Grated cheeses to taste
Chopped herbs to taste

Dissolve the yeast in the water in a large bowl. Let stand until the mixture is foamy. Add the olive oil and bread flour and mix well. Add the sugar, salt, olives, bell pepper, garlic, herbs and red chiles and mix until a dough forms, adding additional water or bread flour to achieve the desired consistency. You may mix in an electric mixer, using the dough hook attachment, for 7 to 10 minutes or until the dough holds together and is of the desired consistency.

Let rise, covered with a warm damp cloth, for 20 to 30 minutes or until doubled in bulk. Stretch the dough on a lightly greased 12×16-inch baking sheet, dimpling the dough with your fingertips to help spread it evenly in the pan. Top with sautéed vegetables, grated cheeses and chopped herbs. Bake at 350 degrees for 15 to 20 minutes or until golden brown. Slice and serve.

*Yield: 16 servings*

 *Bake Shop at Sandestin*

# Stuffed Focaccia Pie

1 recipe Homemade Focaccia dough
  (above)
Chopped Capacola ham or
  prosciutto to taste

Sautéed vegetables to taste
Fresh mozzarella cheese slices to taste
Chopped fresh herbs to taste

Press the desired portion of the Homemade Focaccia dough into a round on a lightly floured surface. Layer with ham, vegetables, cheese and herbs. Fold the dough to form a semicircle. Place the stuffed focaccia pocket in a lightly greased pie plate or round baking dish, pressing gently with your fingertips to spread the pocket evenly in the pan. Bake at 350 degrees for 15 to 20 minutes or until golden brown. Remove from the pan. Slice and serve.

*Yield: variable*

*Bake Shop at Sandestin*

# Asparagus Soup with Crab

*A beautiful green soup with the pure taste of fresh asparagus. The crab is added at the last moment as a luxurious garnish.*

3 to 3½ pounds fresh asparagus
2 tablespoons butter
6 cups chicken stock
Salt and freshly ground pepper to taste
2 tablespoons cornstarch
2 to 3 tablespoons cold water
½ cup whipping cream
6 to 7 ounces white crabmeat, shells removed and flaked

Trim the woody ends from the bottom of the asparagus spears and cut the spears into 1-inch pieces. Melt the butter in a heavy saucepan over medium-high heat. Cook the asparagus in the butter for 5 to 6 minutes or until bright green, stirring frequently. Add the stock and bring to a boil over high heat, skimming off any foam that rises to the surface.

Reduce the heat. Simmer over medium heat for 3 to 5 minutes or until the asparagus is tender-crisp. Reserve 12 to 16 asparagus tips. Season the soup with salt and pepper. Simmer, covered, for 15 to 20 minutes or until the asparagus is very tender.

Purée the soup in a blender or food processor. Strain the soup into the saucepan through a fine sieve. Bring to a boil over medium-high heat. Blend the cornstarch with the water in a small cup. Whisk the cornstarch mixture into the boiling soup, stirring until the soup is thickened. Stir in the cream and adjust the seasonings. Ladle into soup bowls and top each with a spoonful of the crabmeat. Sprinkle with the reserved asparagus tips.

*Yield: 6 to 8 servings*

*Bijoux Bistro*

# Quick Summer Soup for the Beach

1 (46-ounce) can vegetable juice cocktail
1/2 cup sour cream
1 to 2 teaspoons grated onion
1 tablespoon Worcestershire sauce
4 to 6 teaspoons sour cream

Combine the vegetable juice cocktail, 1/2 cup sour cream, onion and Worcestershire sauce in a blender and process until smooth. Refrigerate, covered, for 2 hours or longer. Pour into individual soup bowls and top each serving with 1 teaspoon sour cream. Garnish with chopped fresh chives or dill weed.

*Yield: 4 to 6 servings*

# Corn Chowder

6 slices bacon
1 medium onion, chopped
2 to 3 medium potatoes, peeled, cubed
1/2 cup water
2 cups milk
1 (17-ounce) can cream-style corn
1/2 teaspoon salt
Pepper to taste

Cook the bacon in a large saucepan until crisp. Drain on paper towels, reserving the drippings in the pan. Sauté the onion in the bacon drippings until tender. Add the potatoes and water and stir to mix. Simmer, covered, for 15 to 20 minutes or until the potatoes are tender. Stir in the milk, corn, salt and pepper. Cook over medium heat until heated through, stirring frequently. Crumble the bacon. Ladle the chowder into soup bowls and sprinkle each serving with some of the bacon.

*Yield: 4 to 6 servings*

# Gazpacho

*I love soup, almost any kind and especially homemade. I fell in love with gazpacho on a trip to Mexico City. Since then, I have collected many recipes, but have settled on this one. The best part about gazpacho is the flexibility of the dish. Feel free to substitute the vegetables called for in the tomato base with whatever you find fresh at the market.*

4 large tomatoes, peeled, quartered, seeded

1 cucumber, peeled, quartered, seeded

1 red or green bell pepper, peeled, quartered, seeded

1/2 cup coarsely chopped green onions

1 large garlic clove

2 cups tomato juice, chilled

2 1/2 tablespoons extra-virgin olive oil

2 tablespoons vinegar

1/2 teaspoon salt

1/4 teaspoon black pepper

1/4 teaspoon cayenne pepper

Combine the tomatoes, cucumber, bell pepper, green onions and garlic in a food processor and process until finely chopped but not puréed. Pour into a mixing bowl. Add the tomato juice, olive oil, vinegar, salt, black pepper and cayenne pepper and mix well. Refrigerate, covered, until serving time. Pour into chilled soup bowls. Garnish with croutons or chopped green onions.

*Yield: 4 to 6 servings*

# Marinated Asparagus

*The salt in this dish not only adds flavor, but enhances the bright green color of the asparagus as well.*

| | |
|---|---|
| 1 gallon salted water | 1/2 teaspoon salt |
| 2 bunches asparagus, trimmed | 1/2 teaspoon pepper |
| 1 gallon ice water | 1 garlic clove, minced |
| 2/3 cup olive oil | 1 teaspoon chopped fresh dill weed |
| 1/4 cup white wine vinegar | 1 teaspoon chopped fresh mint |
| Juice of 1 lemon | 1 teaspoon chopped fresh parsley |

Bring the salted water to a boil in a large stockpot. Add the asparagus and cook for 1 to 2 minutes; drain. Plunge the asparagus immediately into the ice water in a bowl to stop the cooking process. Combine the olive oil, vinegar, lemon juice, salt, pepper, garlic, dill weed, mint and parsley in a bowl and whisk to blend. Drain the asparagus and place in a shallow dish. Pour the dressing over the asparagus. Marinate, covered, for 30 minutes to 2 hours depending on the concentration of flavor desired.

*Note:* The longer the asparagus marinates, the greater the loss of the bright green color.

*Yield: 6 to 8 servings*

# Roasted Vegetables

| | |
|---|---|
| 1 pound portobello mushrooms | 3 sprigs of fresh rosemary |
| Trimmed asparagus to taste, cut into 2-inch lengths | 3 sprigs of fresh thyme |
| Peeled carrots to taste, sliced or julienned | 3 tablespoons balsamic vinegar |
| | 3 tablespoons olive oil |
| Thinly sliced peeled potatoes to taste (optional) | Salt and pepper to taste |

Combine the mushrooms, asparagus, carrots, potatoes, rosemary sprigs and thyme sprigs in a large sealable plastic bag. Combine the vinegar, olive oil, salt and pepper in a small bowl and whisk to blend. Pour over the vegetables in the bag. Seal the bag and shake to coat the ingredients. Place the vegetables on a lightly greased baking sheet. Roast at 425 degrees for 15 to 25 minutes or until done to taste, stirring once.

*Yield: variable*

# Seafood Quiche

*This is great for a brunch or dinner and the leftovers are good served cold.*

1 cup chopped mixed fresh seafood, such as crab and lobster
1 unbaked (9-inch) pie shell
4 ounces Swiss cheese, chopped
1/2 cup sliced fresh mushrooms
3 eggs, beaten
1 1/2 cups half-and-half
Nutmeg to taste
Salt and pepper to taste

Arrange the seafood over the bottom of the pie shell. Layer with the cheese and mushrooms. Combine the eggs, half-and-half, nutmeg, salt and pepper in a bowl and beat until blended. Pour over the prepared layers. Bake at 375 degrees for 25 to 35 minutes or until set. Cool on a wire rack.

*Yield: 6 to 8 servings*

# Crabmeat Loaf

1 (10-ounce) can cream of mushroom soup
1 tablespoon unflavored gelatin
3 tablespoons water
8 ounces cream cheese, softened
1 cup mayonnaise
1 (6-ounce) can crabmeat, shells removed and flaked
1 bunch green onions, chopped
1 cup chopped celery
1 tablespoon lemon juice

Heat the soup in a large saucepan. Dissolve the gelatin in the water in a small bowl. Add to the soup, stirring to mix. Remove from the heat and let stand to cool slightly. Combine the cream cheese and mayonnaise in a bowl and mix well. Add to the soup mixture and stir to mix. Stir in the crabmeat, green onions, celery and lemon juice. Pour into a greased 5- to 6-cup loaf-shaped gelatin mold. Refrigerate, covered, overnight or until firm. Unmold onto a serving platter.

*Yield: 8 servings*

Afternoon Mixers

# Swamp Breeze

1 (6-ounce) can frozen limeade concentrate
1 cup spiced rum
3/4 cup dark rum
1/3 cup orange liqueur
Ice cubes
2 or 3 sprigs of fresh mint

Combine the limeade concentrate, spiced rum, dark rum and orange liqueur in a blender and process until smooth. Add enough ice cubes to reach the 5-cup mark on the blender container. Process until smooth. Pour into glasses and garnish with additional fresh mint sprigs.

*Yield: 5 cups*

# Yuca

*This is an especially fun concoction for a beach gathering. All partakers of the potion should participate in the "shaking of the jar."*

8 lemons, cut into quarters
4 limes, cut into quarters
1 (heaping) cup sugar
1 fifth vodka, preferably Skyy
Crushed ice

Squeeze and drop the lemon and lime quarters into a very large clean pickle jar with a tight-fitting lid. Add the sugar and vodka. Add crushed ice until the jar is completely full. Place the lid on the jar and wrap the jar in a towel. Shake the jar for 15 to 20 minutes or until half the ice has melted.

*Yield: 6 to 8 servings*

## Pitcher Bloody Marys

1 (46-ounce) can tomato juice
1 cup vodka
Juice of 2 lemons
2 tablespoons Worcestershire sauce
1/2 teaspoon hot red pepper sauce
1/4 teaspoon pepper
1/8 teaspoon celery seeds
1 tablespoon salt

Combine the tomato juice, vodka, lemon juice, Worcestershire sauce, hot red pepper sauce, pepper, celery seeds and salt in a large pitcher and stir to mix. Serve over ice in glasses. Garnish with celery sticks. Prepare ahead if possible to allow the flavors to blend.

*Yield: 1³/4 quarts*


## Springtime Punch

2 cups sugar
2¹/2 cups water
1 cup fresh lemon juice (3 to 4 lemons)
1 cup fresh orange juice (2 to 3 oranges)
1 (6-ounce) can frozen pineapple juice concentrate, thawed
2 quarts ginger ale, chilled

Combine the sugar and water in a saucepan and mix well. Bring to a boil over high heat. Boil for 10 minutes, stirring frequently. Remove from the heat. Stir in the lemon juice, orange juice and pineapple juice concentrate. Refrigerate, covered, until serving time. Pour into a punch bowl and add the ginger ale. Stir to mix.

*Yield: 16 to 20 servings*

## Fruity Tea

2 quarts boiling water
4 tea bags
2 mint tea bags
1 cup sugar
1 (6-ounce) can frozen lemonade concentrate, thawed
1 (6-ounce) can frozen orange juice concentrate, thawed
1 cup pineapple juice

Pour the boiling water into a 3-quart heatproof pitcher. Add the tea bags and steep for 10 minutes. Remove and discard the tea bags. Add the sugar, stirring until dissolved. Let stand until cool. Add the lemonade concentrate, orange juice concentrate and pineapple juice and stir until well mixed. Serve over ice in glasses.

*Yield: (about) 3 quarts*

## Lemon Almond Tea

4 cups strong brewed tea
3 1/4 cups water
1 (6-ounce) can frozen lemonade concentrate, thawed
1 cup sugar
1/2 teaspoon almond extract

Combine the tea, water, lemonade concentrate, sugar and almond extract in a large pitcher and stir until the sugar is dissolved and the mixture is well blended. Serve over ice in glasses.

*Yield: (about) 2 1/2 quarts*

# Tomato Mozzarella Salad

2 large tomatoes, seeded, cubed
8 ounces mozzarella cheese, cubed
1/4 cup chopped onion
3 tablespoons vegetable oil

2 tablespoons lemon juice
1 1/2 teaspoons basil
1/2 teaspoon salt
Dash of pepper

Combine the tomatoes, cheese, onion, oil, lemon juice, basil, salt and pepper in a medium bowl and mix well. Refrigerate, covered, for 2 hours or longer.

*Yield: 4 servings*

# Salad Niçoise

ANCHOVY DRESSING
1/2 cup plus 1 tablespoon red wine
   vinegar
3 tablespoons Dijon mustard
1 tablespoon anchovy paste

1 1/2 teaspoons thyme, crumbled
Salt and pepper to taste
1 cup olive oil

GREEN BEAN AND POTATO SALAD
3 cups fresh green beans, blanched
6 to 8 small red potatoes, boiled,
   sliced
1 1/2 heads Boston lettuce, washed,
   spun dry

12 cherry tomatoes
2 hard-cooked eggs, sliced
3 (6-ounce) tuna fillets, seared, sliced,
   or 3 (6-ounce) cans albacore tuna,
   drained

**For the dressing,** combine the vinegar, Dijon mustard, anchovy paste, thyme, salt and pepper in a bowl and whisk to blend. Add the olive oil in a fine stream, whisking constantly until blended.

**For the salad,** toss the green beans and potatoes with enough of the dressing to coat in a bowl. Layer the lettuce, tomatoes, green bean mixture, eggs and tuna on a serving plate. Drizzle with the remaining dressing and garnish with niçoise olives.

**Note:** You may substitute another favorite lettuce for the Boston lettuce.

*Yield: 6 to 8 servings*

# Sherried Chicken and Grape Salad

6 cups chopped cooked chicken
3 cups sliced green seedless grapes
1 cup slivered almonds, toasted
2 ribs celery, chopped
3 green onions, minced
3/4 cup mayonnaise

1/4 cup sour cream
2 tablespoons sherry
1/2 teaspoon seasoned salt
1/2 teaspoon seasoned pepper

Combine the chicken, grapes, almonds, celery and green onions in a large bowl and toss to mix. Combine the mayonnaise, sour cream, wine, seasoned salt and seasoned pepper in a small bowl and whisk to blend. Pour the dressing over the salad and toss to coat. Spoon into a serving bowl.

*Yield: 6 servings*

## Memories

Barbara and Dale Nelson live on the Raven Golf Course and relate that one of the joys of their location is just looking out their kitchen window. Recently as they looked across the golf course by the 18th green they saw three deer eating grass. On their nightly walks they've seen coyotes and even a fox.

# Oyster Salad

1 gallon oysters

1 large bottle Italian salad dressing

2 teaspoons olive oil

Juice of 1 lemon

1/2 cup dry wine

2 teaspoons vinegar

6 large onions, finely chopped

1 garlic bulb, finely chopped

Tabasco sauce to taste

Salt and pepper to taste

Drain the oysters, reserving 2 tablespoons of the liquid. Combine the oysters, salad dressing, olive oil, lemon juice, wine, vinegar, reserved liquid, onions, garlic, Tabasco sauce, salt and pepper in a large bowl and mix well. Refrigerate, covered, for 2 hours or longer.

*Note:* The longer the mixture marinates, the better it will taste.

*Yield: 10 to 12 servings*

# Grilled Oysters

24 fresh oysters in the shell

4 ounces applewood bacon, cut into
   1/4-inch strips

1 small Vidalia onion, chopped

2 tablespoons brown sugar

2 garlic cloves, finely chopped

Salt and pepper to taste

2 bunches fresh spinach, rinsed,
   stemmed

Juice of 2 lemons

Grated Romano cheese to taste

Shuck the oysters and rinse to remove any excess shell from around the edges. Leave the muscle attached to the shell underneath each oyster. Cook the bacon in a hot sauté pan until crisp. Drain on paper towels, reserving the drippings in the pan. Crumble the bacon. Sauté the onion in the drippings over high heat. Stir in the brown sugar, garlic, salt and pepper. Sauté the mixture until the onion is caramelized. Add the spinach, bacon and lemon juice and mix well. Cook over high heat until the spinach is wilted, stirring constantly. Divide the mixture evenly among the 24 oysters. Sprinkle each with grated cheese. Arrange the oysters carefully on a preheated grill rack over an open flame. Close the grill lid. Grill for 6 to 8 minutes over high heat. Remove the oysters carefully to a serving platter.

*Yield: 6 to 8 servings*

# Spinach Madeline

2 (10-ounce) packages frozen
  chopped spinach
1/4 cup (1/2 stick) butter
2 tablespoons flour
2 tablespoons chopped onion
1/2 cup evaporated milk
3/4 teaspoon celery salt

3/4 teaspoon garlic salt
1/2 teaspoon salt
1/2 teaspoon black pepper
Ground red pepper to taste
  (cayenne)
1 (6-ounce) roll jalapeño cheese
1 teaspoon Worcestershire sauce

Cook the spinach using the package directions. Drain, reserving 1/2 cup of the cooking liquid. Melt the butter in a saucepan. Add the flour, onion, evaporated milk and reserved liquid and mix well. Cook until thickened, stirring constantly. Add the celery salt, garlic salt, salt, black pepper, red pepper, cheese and Worcestershire sauce and stir until the cheese is melted. Combine the sauce with the spinach in a bowl and mix well. Spoon into a serving dish and serve hot as a dip or with fresh uncooked oysters. You may freeze any leftovers.

*Note:* To serve as a vegetable side dish, spoon the mixture into a baking dish, sprinkle with grated Parmesan cheese and heat in the oven until the cheese melts.

*Yield: (about) 3 cups dip*

## Memories

When asked for her earliest memories of Sandestin, Betty Main's voice becomes even more animated than usual. "Johnny and I were in hog heaven!" she says. "We had the place all to ourselves. Most of the time there was hardly anyone else here. Bob Hope came every year to play golf." Back then, when you looked around, all you saw was the Links Course and the Bay. Betty and Johnny were one of the thirteen original couples. They have celebrated four generations of birthdays at Sandestin, and look forward to many more.

# Baked Scallops Appetizer

*This makes a wonderful appetizer, or it can be served as an entrée with a fresh salad and bread selected from a local bakery. It makes a nice change from shrimp for visitors and local friends.*

18 to 24 large sea scallops
Salt and pepper to taste
1/3 cup butter, softened
1 teaspoon fresh lemon juice
1/2 teaspoon parsley flakes
1/4 teaspoon minced onion
1/4 teaspoon garlic powder
1/4 cup bread crumbs or crushed butter crackers (optional)
6 lemon wedges

Arrange 3 or 4 scallops in each of 6 scalloped baking shells. Sprinkle with salt and pepper. Combine the butter, lemon juice, parsley, onion and garlic powder in a bowl and mix well. Top each prepared shell with 1 rounded teaspoon of the butter mixture. Sprinkle evenly with the bread crumbs. Place the prepared shells on a baking sheet. Bake at 425 degrees for 10 to 15 minutes or until the butter mixture is melted and the scallops are cooked through and hot. Arrange the shells on a serving platter and top each with 1 lemon wedge. Serve immediately.

*Note:* If you don't have scalloped baking shells, you may bake the recipe in a large baking dish following the same procedure as above.

*Yield: 6 servings*

# Crab Canapés

1 cup mayonnaise
1/2 cup shredded sharp Cheddar cheese
1/4 cup chopped green onions
1 (4-ounce) can crabmeat, drained
4 English muffins, split, cut into quarters

Combine the mayonnaise, cheese, green onions and crabmeat in a bowl and mix well. Spread evenly over the English muffin quarters. Arrange on a baking sheet. Broil until bubbly. You may substitute 32 party pumpernickel bread slices for the English muffin quarters.

*Yield: 32 canapés*

# Marinated Shrimp on the Marsh

## LEMON AND CAPER MARINADE

1/2 cup very light vegetable oil

1 cup white wine vinegar

1 teaspoon lemon juice

1/4 cup drained capers

Dash of Tabasco sauce

## BOILED SHRIMP

3/4 cup chopped celery with leaves

1/4 cup mixed pickling spices, or
  1 Old Bay seasoning bag

1 teaspoon salt

2 1/2 pounds fresh shrimp, peeled,
  deveined

2 sweet onions, sliced, separated into
  rings (Texas Sweets or Vidalias are
  recommended)

5 or 6 bay leaves

2 lemons, thinly sliced

*For the marinade,* combine the oil, vinegar, lemon juice, capers and Tabasco sauce in a bowl and mix well.

*For the shrimp,* bring a large pot of water to a rolling boil. Add the celery, pickling spices and salt and boil for 2 minutes. Add the shrimp. Reduce the heat and simmer, covered, for 5 minutes. Drain the shrimp and immediately rinse with cold water. Layer the shrimp, onions, bay leaves and lemons 1/2 at a time in a large glass bowl. Pour the marinade over the prepared layers.

Refrigerate, covered, for 24 hours or longer, stirring several times to be sure all of the shrimp are coated with the marinade. Drain and discard some of the marinade. Discard the bay leaves. Pour the shrimp mixture into a footed trifle bowl. Serve with cocktail forks or fancy tall wooden picks. You may substitute an equal amount of deveined peeled cooked shrimp for the fresh shrimp if desired to save time.

*Note:* Roll whole lemons firmly against the counter with the palm of your hand to loosen the membranes and juice inside before slicing.

*Yield: 6 servings*

# Shrimp Squares

French salad dressing
1 (4-ounce) can small shrimp, drained
1 (5-ounce) jar Old English cheese
½ cup (1 stick) butter, softened
1 small loaf sliced white bread, crusts trimmed

Pour enough salad dressing over the shrimp in a bowl to cover but not saturate all of the shrimp. Marinate, covered, in the refrigerator for several hours. Combine the cheese and butter in a bowl and mix well. Drain the shrimp, discarding the marinade. Add the shrimp to the cheese mixture and mix well. Refrigerate, covered, for 1 hour. Cut each bread slice into quarters and arrange on a baking sheet. Toast in the oven until crisp but not brown.

Spread the shrimp mixture generously over the toast squares, covering the toast completely. Broil for 5 to 6 minutes or until brown and bubbly, watching carefully to prevent burning. Serve immediately. You may prepare the squares several hours ahead. Refrigerate on waxed paper until ready to broil. Return the squares to the baking sheet and broil as directed.

*Yield: 4 to 5 dozen squares*

# Boiled Shrimp and Sauce

**PICKLED SHRIMP**

8 cups water

1 tablespoon caraway seeds

1 tablespoon pickling spices

1 tablespoon whole peppercorns

4 teaspoons salt

1 bay leaf

1 teaspoon dry mustard

1 teaspoon red pepper (cayenne)

Celery leaves to taste

6 pounds deveined peeled fresh shrimp

**LEMON TARRAGON SAUCE**

Juice of 2 lemons

2 tablespoons soy sauce

1 tablespoon tarragon wine vinegar

1 tablespoon Worcestershire sauce

7 or 8 drops of Tabasco sauce

1 teaspoon salt

1 cup (2 sticks) butter (no substitutions)

**For the shrimp,** bring the water to a boil in a large pot. Add the caraway seeds, pickling spices, peppercorns, salt, bay leaf, dry mustard, red pepper and celery leaves and mix well. Boil for 20 minutes, stirring occasionally. Add the shrimp and cook for 8 minutes or until pink, stirring occasionally. Drain and set aside.

**For the sauce,** combine the lemon juice, soy sauce, vinegar, Worcestershire sauce, Tabasco sauce, salt and butter in a saucepan. Heat until the butter is melted and the mixture is blended, stirring frequently. Pour over the shrimp in a serving bowl.

*Yield: 8 servings*

# Barbecued Jalapeño Shrimp Wraps

*The combination of flavors in these wraps is fabulous.*

12 fresh jalapeño chiles

8 ounces cream cheese

24 medium (26- to 30-count) fresh
  shrimp, peeled

8 slices bacon

Soak 24 wooden picks in water for 1 hour to prevent burning on the grill. Cut the jalapeño chiles in half lengthwise. Remove and discard the seeds and membranes. Fill each half with some of the cream cheese. Top each with 1 shrimp. Cut each bacon slice into thirds. Wrap 1 filled jalapeño chile half completely with 1 bacon piece and secure with 1 wooden pick. Repeat with the remaining ingredients. Arrange the wraps on a hot grill rack shrimp side down over hot coals. Grill until the bacon browns and the shrimp are opaque. Turn the wraps over and grill chile side down until the bacon browns and the drippings flare the fire, leaving burn marks on the chiles. Remove to a platter using tongs. Let stand for 5 minutes before serving.

*Yield: 24 wraps*

# Pickled Shrimp

3 tablespoons pickling spices
1 cup vegetable oil
1/2 cup lemon juice
1/2 cup vinegar
1 teaspoon Worcestershire sauce
2 teaspoons sugar
1 teaspoon salt

3²/3 cups deveined peeled fresh
  shrimp
3/4 cup sweet pickle relish
2 medium onions, sliced
2 hard-cooked eggs, chopped
  (optional)

Tie the pickling spices in cheesecloth. Combine the oil, lemon juice, vinegar, Worcestershire sauce, sugar and salt in a jar with a tight-fitting lid. Shake the jar to mix the ingredients. Combine the shrimp, relish, onions and pickling spices bag in a bowl. Pour the marinade over the shrimp mixture. Refrigerate, covered, for 24 hours or longer. Remove and discard the pickling spice bag. Add the eggs and mix well. Spoon into a serving dish.

*Yield: 8 servings*

# Rémoulade Sauce

1/4 cup lemon juice
1/4 cup mustard
1/4 cup vinegar
1/4 cup horseradish
3 tablespoons ketchup

2 teaspoons salt
2 teaspoons paprika
1/2 teaspoon red pepper (cayenne)
1 cup vegetable oil
3/4 cup chopped green onions

Combine the lemon juice, mustard, vinegar, horseradish, ketchup, salt, paprika and red pepper in a blender and process until smooth. Add the oil in a fine stream, processing constantly until blended. Add the green onions and mix well.

*Yield: (about) 3 cups sauce*

# Chicken Salad Pick-Ups

*These look impressive and will disappear quickly.*

30 frozen phyllo tartlet shells
6 boneless skinless chicken breasts, cooked, chopped
1 (8-ounce) can salted cashew halves
2 medium avocados, chopped
3 tablespoons lemon juice
1 cup mayonnaise or low-fat mayonnaise
1 teaspoon pepper

Bake the tartlet shells using the package directions; cool. Combine the chicken, cashews, avocados, lemon juice, mayonnaise and pepper in a bowl and mix well. Refrigerate, covered, for up to 2 days. Fill the tartlet shells with the chicken salad just before serving. Arrange the shells on a serving platter and garnish with fresh parsley.

*Note:* You may bake, poach or grill the chicken.

*Yield: 30 pick-ups*


# Veggie Bites

*This recipe may be easily halved for a small party.*

2 (8-count) cans crescent rolls
1 egg, beaten
16 ounces cream cheese, softened
1 cup mayonnaise
1 envelope ranch salad dressing mix
1/2 cup each finely chopped broccoli, cauliflower, mushrooms, green bell pepper,
    tomato and black olives
2 to 3 green onions, finely chopped
3/4 cup shredded Cheddar cheese

Unroll the crescent roll dough and press over the bottom of a 10×15-inch baking pan, sealing the perforations. Brush the dough with the egg. Bake at 375 degrees for 11 to 13 minutes. Cool on a wire rack. Beat the cream cheese with the mayonnaise and salad dressing mix in a bowl until smooth. Spread over the cooled crust. Sprinkle evenly with the broccoli, cauliflower, mushrooms, bell pepper, tomato, olives and green onions. Top with the Cheddar cheese. Cut into small squares.

*Note:* You may chop the vegetables in a food processor to save time, but be careful not to chop too finely.

*Yield: 3 to 4 dozen squares*

# Rio Grande Nachos Grande

Vegetable oil for frying
4 (8-inch) flour tortillas
1 (16-ounce) can refried beans
2 cups chopped cooked broccoli
1 cup (4 ounces) shredded Monterey Jack cheese
1 cup (4 ounces) shredded Cheddar cheese
1 cup spicy tomato salsa
Sliced jalapeño chiles to taste
Sliced green onions to taste
1 cup sour cream

Heat 1/2 inch oil in a medium skillet just until it begins to ripple. Fry the tortillas 1 at a time in the hot oil until golden on each side. Drain on paper towels. Arrange the tortillas on a baking sheet. Spread the refried beans evenly over the tortillas. Layer with the broccoli, Monterey Jack cheese, Cheddar cheese and salsa. Top with jalapeño chile slices. Bake at 350 degrees for 15 to 20 minutes or until the cheese melts. Sprinkle with green onion slices and serve. Pass the sour cream on the side.

*Yield: 4 servings*

# Pot Stickers

*These are quite time-consuming to prepare, but assembling and folding the dumplings can be a fun part of your party! Supply each guest with waxed paper and small bowls of water for fingertip dipping. These are also delicious reheated for breakfast.*

## PORK DUMPLINGS

1 (10-ounce) package frozen
   chopped spinach, thawed
24 ounces twice-ground pork (Boston
   butt is suitable for grinding)
1/2 cup chopped fresh gingerroot
1 tablespoon finely chopped fresh
   garlic
1 bunch green onions, finely chopped
1/2 (10-ounce) can cream of
   mushroom soup
3 tablespoons cooking wine
4 eggs, beaten

2 to 3 tablespoons honey
1/4 cup soy sauce
1 teaspoon MSG (optional)
2 teaspoons seasoned salt
2 teaspoons white pepper
2 tablespoons cornstarch
2 tablespoons cold water
2 packages egg roll wrappers
   (available in the produce section)
2 tablespoons vegetable oil
2 to 4 tablespoons water

## DIPPING SAUCE

1/2 cup black soy sauce
1 teaspoon chopped fresh gingerroot
1 teaspoon chopped fresh garlic
1/2 green onion, chopped

1 teaspoon sesame oil
Sugar to taste
Vinegar to taste

**For the dumplings,** drain the spinach, pressing out the excess moisture. Combine the spinach, pork, gingerroot, garlic, green onions, soup, wine, eggs, honey, soy sauce, MSG, seasoned salt and white pepper in a bowl and mix well. Dissolve the cornstarch in 2 tablespoons cold water in a small cup. Add to the spinach mixture and mix well. Refrigerate, covered, for 2 hours or longer.

Cut each egg roll wrapper into quarters. Place a sheet of waxed paper on the work surface next to a bowl of water for wetting fingertips. Lay 1 wrapper quarter on the waxed paper and place 1 small spoonful of the filling in the center. Wet your fingertips lightly and moisten 2 adjacent edges of the wrapper. Do not use too much water, as this will make the dumplings soggy and stick together. Fold the dry corner over to meet the wet corner. Seal the edges thoroughly, forcing the air out of the pocket while sealing. Dampen 1 of the 45-degree corners and fold it over to meet the other on the "belly" of the dumpling, keeping your thumb under the corners. The dumpling should look somewhat like an envelope with the flap open. Repeat the process until all of the filling is used. Arrange the dumplings on a waxed paper-lined baking sheet.

Heat the oil in a large nonstick skillet. Arrange the filled dumplings in a circle slightly overlapping around the outer edge of the pan. Arrange a second ring of dumplings just inside the first ring and so on until the pan is full. Pour 2 to 4 tablespoons water in between the dumplings. Cover the pan with a tight-fitting lid. Cook over medium-high heat for 7 minutes or until the egg roll wrappers are translucent. (The water steams the pork filling while the oil fries the wrapper bottoms.) Do not flip the dumplings, as they should be soft on the top and crispy on the bottom. Test for doneness by opening 1 dumpling to make sure the pork is cooked through. Remove from the pan and keep warm.

*For the sauce*, combine the soy sauce, gingerroot, garlic, green onion, sesame oil, sugar and vinegar in a bowl and mix well. Pour into a serving bowl. Serve the pot stickers with the dipping sauce.

*Note:* You may prepare the filling ahead and freeze it alone, or freeze the filled and cooked dumplings, making sure the dumplings do not touch.

*Yield: 10 to 15 servings*

## Memories

*Allison Yii's father arrived in the United States from Sichuan, China, in 1949 with just a suitcase to his name. He did not have any of his recipes with him and he soon discovered how much he missed his "home-province" cooking. Thus, attempting to recreate some of the tastes from home he came up with this recipe for Guotea (pot stickers). Guotea has been a part of Allison's family as long as she can remember. She says that after working at Sandestin for seventeen years, she considers it an honor to share her family's recipe with her Sandestin family.*

# Mushroom Croustades

## BREAD SHELLS

2 tablespoons butter, softened
24 thin slices fresh white bread, crusts trimmed

## MUSHROOM FILLING

1/4 cup (1/2 stick) butter
3 tablespoons finely chopped shallots
8 ounces fresh mushrooms, finely
  chopped
2 tablespoons flour
1 cup heavy cream
1/2 teaspoon lemon juice
1 tablespoon finely chopped fresh
  parsley

1 1/2 teaspoons finely chopped fresh
  chives
Pinch of salt
Pinch of black pepper
Pinch of cayenne pepper
2 tablespoons grated Parmesan
  cheese
Butter

*For the shells,* coat 24 miniature muffin cups with the butter. Cut a 3-inch round from each bread slice using a biscuit cutter. Line each prepared muffin cup with 1 bread round, pressing to shape into a cup. Bake at 400 degrees for 10 minutes or until light brown. Remove from the pan. Cool on a wire rack. You may freeze the shells for later use.

*For the filling,* melt 1/4 cup butter in a large sauté pan. Cook the shallots in the butter for 3 minutes. Add the mushrooms and cook for 15 minutes or until the moisture has evaporated, stirring constantly. Remove from the heat. Stir in the flour. Pour the cream over the mixture. Return to the heat. Bring to a boil and cook until thickened, stirring constantly. Reduce the heat and simmer for 1 to 2 minutes longer. Remove from the heat. Add the lemon juice, parsley, chives, salt, black pepper and cayenne pepper and mix well. Let stand until cool. You may freeze the mixture at this point for later use.

*To serve,* fill the baked shells evenly with the filling. Sprinkle each lightly with some of the Parmesan cheese and dot each with butter. Arrange on a baking sheet. Bake at 350 degrees for 10 minutes.

*Yield: 24 croustades*

# Onion Tartlets

*These freeze very well and are great to keep on hand for a quick appetizer.*

3 slices bacon, finely chopped
2 pounds yellow onions, thinly sliced
1 teaspoon sugar
½ teaspoon salt
2 to 3 teaspoons balsamic
   vinegar

2 to 3 tablespoons chopped fresh
   rosemary or sage
Freshly ground pepper to taste
½ cup half-and-half or heavy cream
2 eggs
30 frozen phyllo tartlet shells

Cook the bacon in a large saucepan until almost crisp. Add the onions, sugar and salt and mix well. Cook for 10 minutes or until the volume is reduced by 2/3, stirring frequently. Add 2 teaspoons of the vinegar and reduce the heat to medium-low. Cook for 15 to 30 minutes or until the onions are evenly golden brown and of a marmalade consistency, stirring frequently and scraping any browned bits from the bottom of the pan. Stir in the rosemary. Cool slightly. Season with pepper. Add the remaining vinegar if the mixture is too sweet. Stir in the half-and-half and eggs. Arrange the tartlet shells on a baking sheet and fill evenly with the onion mixture. Bake at 350 degrees for 15 minutes or until set.

*Note:* This recipe makes more than enough filling for the tartlet shells. Spread the extra onion mixture over French bread slices that have been drizzled with olive oil and toasted in the oven.

*Yield: 30 tartlets*

# Spinach Rockefeller

2 (10-ounce) packages frozen
   chopped spinach
½ cup dry bread crumbs
¼ cup minced green onions
2 eggs, lightly beaten
¼ cup (½ stick) butter, melted
¼ cup grated Parmesan cheese

½ teaspoon minced garlic
½ teaspoon thyme
¼ teaspoon salt
⅛ teaspoon pepper
6 to 8 tomatoes, cut into ¼-inch slices
Garlic salt to taste

Cook the spinach using the package directions; drain well. Combine the spinach, bread crumbs, green onions, eggs, butter, cheese, garlic, thyme, salt and pepper in a bowl and mix well. Arrange the tomato slices in a 2-quart baking dish. Sprinkle with garlic salt. Mound ¼ cup of the spinach mixture onto each tomato slice, shaping each top into a dome. Bake at 350 degrees for 15 to 20 minutes or until set.

*Yield: (about) 15 servings*

# Cheese Straws

1 sheet puff pastry dough
1 egg, beaten
1/2 cup shredded cheese

Cut the puff pastry dough into halves crosswise. Cut each half into thin strips. Brush with the beaten egg. Sprinkle with the cheese. Twist each strip and arrange on a baking sheet. Bake at 400 degrees for about 20 minutes.

*Yield: 20 straws*

# Cocktail Cheese Bites

2 cups flour
8 ounces sharp Cheddar cheese, shredded
8 ounces extra-sharp Cheddar cheese, shredded
1 cup (2 sticks) butter, softened
2 dashes of cayenne pepper
2 cups crisp rice cereal

Combine the flour, sharp Cheddar cheese, extra-sharp Cheddar cheese and butter in a bowl and mix well. Add the cayenne pepper and cereal and mix well. Shape into a log. Refrigerate, wrapped in plastic wrap, until ready to bake. Cut the log into slices and arrange on a baking sheet. Bake at 350 degrees for 10 minutes or until golden brown. Serve hot or cold.

*Note:* After shaping into a log, the dough can be wrapped and frozen for a long period of time. Slice and bake as needed.

*Yield: 4 dozen bites*

# Spicy Cheese Wafers

4 ounces Old English or extra-sharp Cheddar cheese,
  shredded, softened
1/2 cup (1 stick) butter, softened
1 1/4 cups sifted flour
Salt to taste
1/2 teaspoon red pepper (cayenne)
1 cup chopped pecans

Combine the cheese and butter in a mixing bowl and beat until smooth. Combine the flour, salt and red pepper in a bowl and mix well. Add to the cheese mixture and beat until blended. Fold in the pecans. Shape the dough into a log. Refrigerate, wrapped in plastic wrap, for 24 hours. Slice into thin wafers and arrange on a greased baking sheet. Bake at 300 degrees until light brown.

*Yield: 3 dozen wafers*

# Pâté de Foie Campagnarde

8 ounces thinly sliced bacon

1 onion, finely chopped

1 tablespoon butter

1/2 cup heavy cream

12 ounces chicken livers

1 pound ground pork

8 ounces ground veal

2 garlic cloves, crushed

1/4 teaspoon allspice

Pinch of ground cloves

Pinch of nutmeg

2 eggs, beaten

2 tablespoons Cognac or Calvados

Salt and pepper to taste

1/2 cup pistachios or hazelnuts, chopped (optional)

8 ounces ham, cut into strips

1 bay leaf

1 sprig of fresh thyme

Line a 2-quart terrine with the bacon, allowing the slices to hang over the edges. Sauté the onion in the butter in a skillet until tender. Bring the cream to a boil in a saucepan. Add the chicken livers and poach for 3 minutes. Remove from the heat. Drain the chicken livers, reserving the cream. Purée the chicken livers in a food processor. Combine the onion mixture, chicken livers, ground pork, ground veal, garlic, allspice, cloves, nutmeg, eggs, reserved cream, Cognac and a generous amount of salt and pepper in a large bowl and mix well. The mixture should be strongly seasoned, since the terrine is served cold and the flavors are therefore diminished. Stir in the pistachios.

Spread 1/3 of the pork mixture in the prepared terrine and press down with wet fingers. Layer evenly with 1/2 of the ham strips and 1/2 of the remaining onion mixture. Top with the remaining ham strips and pork mixture. Place the bay leaf and thyme sprig on the top and fold the bacon strips over the top. Cover with a tight-fitting lid seal tightly with foil. Set the terrine inside a larger pan filled halfway with water. Bake at 350 degrees for 1 1/2 hours. Remove the terrine to a wire rack to cool. Remove the lid or foil and place weights over the top of the baked layers. Refrigerate, covered, for several days to allow the flavors to mellow before serving. Unmold onto a serving platter and cut into slices. Serve with cornichons, Dijon mustard and French bread.

*Yield: 8 to 10 servings*

# Smoked Salmon Pâté

1 (16-ounce) can pink salmon, drained
8 ounces cream cheese, softened
2 tablespoons chopped green onions,
    or 1 tablespoon dried minced onion
1/4 teaspoon salt
1/4 teaspoon pepper
1 tablespoon lemon juice
1 tablespoon liquid smoke
1 teaspoon prepared horseradish

Discard any skin and bones from the salmon and flake the salmon with a fork.
Combine the salmon, cream cheese, green onions, salt, pepper, lemon juice, liquid
smoke and horseradish in a bowl and mix well. Refrigerate, covered, for several hours.
Shape the mixture into a ball or other desired shape and place on a serving plate.
Garnish with chopped nuts, parsley or paprika. Serve with crackers or bagels.

*Note:* You may forgo shaping the pâté and simply spoon the mixture into a decorative
serving dish. Surround the dish with crackers or bagels and serve immediately.

*Yield: 2 cups pâté*

## Memories

*The two things that Ewell Garrett loves the most are
golf and fishing, which is why he and his wife,
Jackie, fell in love with their Fairways townhome
overlooking the lake. If Ewell isn't teeing off, you can
find him sitting on their dock with a fishing rod in hand,
waiting for the "big one." He often spoke of a
"101-pound" bass in the lake, nicknamed "Old Henry."
To Ewell's dismay, "Old Henry" had always gotten
away. However, late one afternoon, Ewell felt a
sudden smack—"Old Henry" was back! Ewell hung on
and this time "Old Henry" was his, all 81 pounds,
10 ounces, of him. There Ewell stood, holding up his
prize catch to the world, but no one was around to see
it. Finally, Jackie returned, and took a picture of the
dynamic duo and to this day that picture hangs on
their wall. "Old Henry" was released and is still
believed to be camera shy.*

# Artichoke Dip

*Warning: This is habit-forming.*

1 cup grated Parmesan cheese
1 cup mayonnaise (no substitutions)
1 cup chopped drained canned artichoke hearts
Garlic powder to taste

Combine the cheese, mayonnaise, artichokes and garlic powder in a bowl and mix well. Spoon into a baking dish. Bake at 350 degrees for 20 to 30 minutes or until bubbly. Cool on a wire rack. Serve with crackers.

*Yield: 3 cups dip*

# Tomato and Artichoke Dip

1/2 cup oil-pack sun-dried tomatoes
1 (14-ounce) can artichoke hearts, drained, chopped
2 cups (8 ounces) shredded Swiss cheese
1/2 cup sour cream
1/4 cup mayonnaise or mayonnaise-type salad dressing
1 teaspoon minced garlic
2 tablespoons grated Parmesan cheese

Drain the tomatoes thoroughly on paper towels. Chop or snip the tomatoes with kitchen scissors. Combine the tomatoes, artichokes, Swiss cheese, sour cream, mayonnaise and garlic in a medium bowl and mix well. Spoon into an 8-inch quiche pan or shallow baking dish and sprinkle with the Parmesan cheese. Bake at 350 degrees for 20 to 25 minutes or until the Swiss cheese is melted. Serve with breadsticks or crackers.

*Yield: (about) 4 cups dip*

# Tuscan Bean Dip

1 (15-ounce) can navy beans, rinsed, drained
2 tablespoons chopped onion
2 tablespoons pesto
1 tablespoon vinegar
1 garlic clove, minced
1/2 to 1 teaspoon finely chopped fresh chile pepper (red or green)
1/4 teaspoon salt

Combine the beans, onion, pesto, vinegar, garlic, chile pepper and salt in a food processor and process until almost smooth. Refrigerate, covered, for several hours or overnight. Stir and pour into a serving dish.

*Yield: 1 1/3 cups dip*

# Mexican Corn Dip

2 (11-ounce) cans Mexicorn, drained
2 cups (8 ounces) shredded Cheddar cheese
1 cup mayonnaise
1 cup sour cream
1 can tomatoes with green chiles, drained

Combine the Mexicorn, cheese, mayonnaise, sour cream and tomatoes with green chiles in a large bowl and mix well. Spoon into a serving dish. Serve with corn chip scoops. May substitute two (4-ounce) cans drained chopped green chiles for the tomatoes with green chiles for a spicier dip.

*Yield: (about) 6 cups dip*

# Curry Dip

*This is a very easy and popular beginning for a dinner party and is also a great "bring-a-dish" contribution.*

1 cup mayonnaise
1 cup sour cream
1 small envelope Italian salad dressing mix
1 teaspoon curry powder
1/2 teaspoon thyme
1/2 teaspoon garlic salt
4 teaspoons vinegar
4 teaspoons vegetable oil

Combine the mayonnaise, sour cream, salad dressing mix, curry powder, thyme, garlic salt, vinegar and oil in a bowl and whisk to blend. Refrigerate in an airtight container for several hours or overnight. Serve with bite-size fresh vegetables.

*Note:* The flavor of the dip improves with time.

*Yield: (about) 4 1/2 cups dip*

# Goat Cheese Dip

12 ounces cream cheese, softened
4 ounces goat cheese (chèvre)
1 large onion, chopped
3 tablespoons olive oil
1 (15-ounce) can diced tomatoes
1/2 cup water
1 teaspoon salt
1 teaspoon pepper

Combine the cream cheese and goat cheese in a bowl and mix well. Spoon into a baking dish. Bake at 350 degrees for 20 minutes. Cool on a wire rack. Sauté the onion in the olive oil in a skillet until tender. Add the undrained tomatoes, water, salt and pepper and stir to mix. Simmer for 20 minutes. Spoon the onion mixture over the top of the baked cheese mixture. Serve with toasted bread.

*Yield: (about) 4 cups dip*

# Cheese Fondue

1 garlic clove, cut into halves
1 1/2 cups dry white wine (preferably chablis)
16 ounces (4 cups) shredded Swiss cheese or a combination of cheeses
3 tablespoons kirsch (clear cherry brandy)

Rub the inside of a fondue pot or crock all over with the cut sides of the garlic halves. Discard the garlic. Add the wine and heat the fondue pot. Add the cheese 1 handful at a time, stirring with a wooden spoon in a figure-eight pattern after each addition, until all of the cheese is melted. Do not add all of the cheese at once. Add the kirsch and stir to mix. Serve with French or Italian bread cubes and fresh apple and pear slices for dipping.

*Note:* When cubing the French or Italian bread, be sure each cube has some crust still attached.

*Yield: (about) 5 1/2 cups fondue*

# Emerald Coast Guacamole

3 ripe avocados
3 tablespoons fresh lemon juice
1 medium tomato, chopped
1/2 cup chopped onion
2 tablespoons minced fresh cilantro
1/2 teaspoon salt

Cut the avocados into halves and remove and discard the pits. Scoop the pulp into a bowl. Drizzle with the lemon juice and mash the avocado pulp with a fork. Add the tomato, onion, cilantro and salt and mix well. Spoon into a serving dish. Serve with tortilla chips.

*Yield: (about) 3 cups dip*

# Chick-Pea Hummus

2 (15-ounce) cans chick-peas (garbanzo beans), rinsed, drained
Juice of 1 lime
2 garlic cloves, finely chopped
1 bunch cilantro, coarsely chopped
Dash of Tabasco sauce
Dash of cumin
1 cup olive oil
Salt and pepper to taste

Combine the chick-peas, lime juice, garlic, cilantro, Tabasco sauce and cumin in a food processor and process until puréed. Add the olive oil in a fine stream, processing constantly until blended and adding water if necessary to achieve the desired consistency. Season with salt and pepper. Spoon into a serving dish. Serve with lavash (Italian cracker bread).

*Yield: (about) 4 cups dip*

# Layered Fiesta Dip

1 envelope taco seasoning mix
1 pound lean ground beef
3/4 cup water
1 (11-ounce) jar refried beans
1/2 cup shredded sharp Cheddar
  cheese
1 (2-ounce) can sliced black olives,
  drained

1 medium tomato, chopped
1 large avocado, coarsely mashed
1/2 cup sour cream
3/4 cup medium-spicy chunky salsa
1/4 cup thinly sliced green onions
1/2 cup shredded sharp Cheddar
  cheese

Prepare the taco seasoning mix with the ground beef and water in a medium skillet using the package directions. Add the beans and heat for 5 minutes, stirring frequently. Spread the cooked beef mixture in a shallow 1-quart serving dish. Layer evenly with 1/2 cup cheese, the olives, tomato, avocado, sour cream, salsa and green onions. Top with 1/2 cup cheese. Serve immediately with nacho chips for dipping.

*Yield: (about) 8 cups dip*

# Venison Bean Dip

1 pound ground venison or sage bulk
  pork sausage
1 small onion, chopped
Butter for sautéing
1 (15-ounce) can kidney beans,
  undrained, mashed

1 teaspoon cayenne pepper
1/2 teaspoon Mexican chili powder
1 (4-ounce) can chopped green chiles
2 (8-ounce) packages sliced Pepper
  Jack cheese

Brown the ground venison in a large skillet, stirring until crumbly; drain. Sauté the onion in a small amount of butter in a skillet until tender. Add the onion mixture to the venison in the skillet and mix well. Combine the beans, cayenne pepper, chili powder and undrained green chiles in a bowl and mix well. Add to the venison mixture and mix well. Simmer over low heat for 20 minutes. Layer the venison mixture and cheese slices 1/2 at a time in a 9×13-inch baking pan. Bake at 350 degrees for 30 minutes. Serve with tortilla or corn chips.

*Note:* Use a disposable lasagna pan for easy transport and/or easy cleanup.

*Yield: (about) 6 cups dip*

# Pineapple Cheese Ball

16 ounces cream cheese, softened
1/2 (8-ounce) can crushed pineapple, well drained
1/4 cup finely chopped green or red bell pepper
2 tablespoons grated onion
1 tablespoon seasoned salt
1 cup chopped pecans

Combine the cream cheese, pineapple, bell pepper, onion and seasoned salt in a bowl and mix well. Shape into a ball. Refrigerate, wrapped in plastic wrap, until firm. Unwrap and roll the cheese ball in the pecans to coat. Refrigerate, covered, until serving time. Serve with crackers.

*Yield: 20 servings*

# Chutney Cheese Ball

8 ounces cream cheese, softened
8 ounces Cheddar cheese, shredded
1 bunch green onions, chopped
1 large jar Major Grey's chutney
1 pound bacon, crisp-cooked, crumbled

Combine the cream cheese and Cheddar cheese in a bowl and mix well. Shape into a ball or log. Refrigerate, covered, overnight. Let stand at room temperature for 3 hours before serving time. Roll the cheese ball in the green onions. Place on a serving plate. Pour the chutney over the top and press the bacon pieces all over the outside of the cheese ball. Serve with wheat crackers.

*Yield: 20 servings*

# Cheddar Nut Ring

*Garnish this attractive ring mold with holly leaves and berries for a festive holiday touch.*

4 cups (16 ounces) shredded sharp Cheddar cheese
1 cup chopped pecans
1 cup mayonnaise
1 small onion, grated, or 1 large bunch green onions, minced
Black pepper to taste
Cayenne pepper to taste
Minced garlic to taste
Raspberry or strawberry jam

Combine the cheese, pecans, mayonnaise, onion, black pepper, cayenne pepper and garlic in a bowl and mix well. Spoon into a greased ring mold. Refrigerate, covered, overnight. Unmold onto a serving plate and fill the opening in the center of the ring with raspberry jam. Serve with crackers.

*Note:* To ease release of the cheese ring from the mold, dip the bottom of the mold in hot water for 2 minutes.

*Yield: 10 to 12 servings*

## Entertaining Hints

*Want an easy way to entertain a large group of people? Consider an hors d'oeuvre party. No chairs, no plates, no cutlery, and, best of all, minimal cleanup. Your food should be tempting to the eye, as well as pleasing to the palate. If food looks fabulous, people will want to sample it. Keep garnishes simple; overdecorated food quickly loses its appeal. Do not overcrowd the serving trays; they tend to look cluttered and messy. Place hors d'oeuvre in neat, evenly spaced rows to maximize their appeal. Present only one or, at most, two kinds of food at a time on a serving tray. Too many choices can be confusing for guests and slow down conversation while they are making decisions.*

# Magnolia & Ivy Tea Spread

8 ounces cream cheese, softened
1/4 cup chopped bell pepper
1/4 cup chopped pimentos
1 tablespoon minced green onions
1/4 cup chopped pecans
2 hard-cooked eggs, grated
2 tablespoons ketchup
Salt and pepper to taste

Combine the cream cheese, bell pepper, pimentos, green onions, pecans, eggs, ketchup, salt and pepper in a bowl and mix well. Refrigerate, covered, overnight. Spread over buttered toast points and garnish with fresh parsley.

For a tea sandwich, spread the mixture between slices of wheat bread.

*Yield: (about) 2 cups spread*

 *Magnolia & Ivy Tearoom*

# Mock Boursin Cheese

24 ounces cream cheese, softened

3/4 cup (1 1/2 sticks) butter, softened

1 (8-ounce) bottle Green Goddess salad dressing

3 to 4 garlic cloves, crushed

Freshly ground pepper to taste

1 or 2 pinches of parsley flakes

Combine the cream cheese, butter, salad dressing, garlic, pepper and parsley in a mixing bowl and beat until well blended. Refrigerate in an airtight container until ready to use. Serve on crackers. You may freeze any leftover cheese mixture.

*Yield: (about) 4 cups spread*

# Bleu Cheese Mold

1 envelope unflavored gelatin

2 tablespoons cool water

1 (10-ounce) can beef consommé

1 tablespoon sherry, vermouth or lemon juice

3 ounces cream cheese, softened

4 ounces crumbled bleu cheese

1 or 2 dashes of Worcestershire sauce

Soften the gelatin in the water in a heatproof bowl. Heat the soup in a small saucepan until hot. Pour over the gelatin and stir until completely dissolved. Cool to lukewarm. Stir in the sherry. Combine the cream cheese and bleu cheese in a bowl and mix with a fork. Add the Worcestershire sauce and mix well. Pour the soup mixture into a greased gelatin mold. Drop the cheese mixture by spoonfuls into the soup mixture in the mold. Refrigerate until set. Unmold onto a serving plate and serve with crackers.

*Yield: 12 to 14 servings*

# Crabmeat Cheese Ball

6 ounces crabmeat, shells removed,
  flaked
8 ounces cream cheese, softened
2 teaspoons chopped fresh chives

1/4 teaspoon salt
1/4 teaspoon garlic powder
Chopped almonds or pecans, toasted

Combine the crabmeat, cream cheese, chives, salt and garlic powder in a bowl and mix well. Shape the mixture into a ball. Roll in chopped almonds and place on a serving plate. Serve with crackers.

*Yield: 4 servings*

# Crabmeat Mold

1 (10-ounce) can cream of mushroom
  soup
1 cup mayonnaise
1 envelope unflavored gelatin
3 tablespoons water
1 pound crabmeat, drained, shells
  removed, flaked

8 ounces cream cheese, softened
1 bunch green onions (white and
  green parts), finely chopped
3 ribs celery, chopped
Parsley flakes to taste
Salt and pepper to taste

Heat the soup in a small saucepan over low heat. Remove from the heat. Stir in the mayonnaise. Dissolve the gelatin in the water in a small cup. Stir into the soup mixture. Add the crabmeat, cream cheese, green onions, celery, parsley, salt and pepper and mix well. Spoon into a lightly greased gelatin mold. Refrigerate, covered, overnight. Unmold onto a serving plate. Serve with assorted crackers.

*Note:* You may substitute 2 cans crabmeat or 2 cans drained shrimp for the crabmeat, or use 1 can of each.

*Yield: 10 to 12 servings*

# Layered Crabmeat Spread

12 ounces cream cheese, softened

1 small onion, grated

2 tablespoons Worcestershire sauce

2 tablespoons mayonnaise

1 tablespoon lemon juice

Dash of garlic salt

1/2 cup chili sauce

6 ounces fresh lump crabmeat, shells removed, flaked, or

1 (6-ounce) can crabmeat, drained, flaked

Combine the cream cheese, onion, Worcestershire sauce, mayonnaise, lemon juice and garlic salt in a mixing bowl and beat until smooth. Spread the mixture evenly in a 12-inch pizza pan. Spread the chili sauce over the top, leaving a 3/4-inch border around the outer edge. Sprinkle with the crabmeat. Refrigerate, covered, until serving time. Garnish with fresh parsley. Serve with crackers. You may use a food processor to blend the cream cheese mixture.

*Note:* You may freeze the cream cheese mixture between two pieces of waxed paper. Peel away the waxed paper and allow the mixture to thaw. Add the sauce and crabmeat just before serving.

*Yield: 3 1/2 cups spread*

## Memories

*Leah and Hiram Hughes purchased their Sandestin property in the early 1980s. At that time the way to the beach was down a dirt road through pine trees and around potholes, but the soft sand and welcome warm waters made it all worthwhile to them and their children.*

## Shrimp Spread

1 cup chopped cooked shrimp
1 tablespoon chopped onion
8 ounces cream cheese, softened
1/2 cup mayonnaise
Dash of curry powder

Combine the shrimp, onion, cream cheese, mayonnaise and curry powder in a bowl and mix well. Refrigerate, covered, for 1 hour or longer to allow the flavors to blend. Serve on crackers.

*Yield: (about) 2½ cups spread*

## Shrimp Salad Mold

1 (3-ounce) package lemon gelatin
1 cup hot water
1 teaspoon lemon juice
1 cup chili sauce
1/4 cup drained horseradish
2 (4-ounce) cans salad shrimp, drained

Combine the gelatin and hot water in a heatproof bowl, stirring until the gelatin is dissolved. Add the lemon juice, chili sauce and horseradish and mix well. Let stand until cool. Add the shrimp and mix well. Spoon into a greased gelatin mold. Refrigerate, covered, until set. Unmold onto a serving plate. Serve with crackers.

*Yield: 6 to 8 servings*

# Shrimp Mousse

2 cups sour cream

16 ounces cream cheese, softened

1 cup mayonnaise

1/2 cup minced bell pepper

1/2 cup minced celery

1/2 cup minced green onions

1/4 cup minced pimentos

1/2 cup chili sauce

1 tablespoon Worcestershire sauce

1/8 teaspoon Tabasco sauce

1 teaspoon salt

2 tablespoons unflavored gelatin

Juice of 2 lemons

1/4 cup cold water

6 cups finely chopped deveined peeled cooked fresh shrimp
(see note)

Cream the sour cream, cream cheese and mayonnaise in a mixing bowl until smooth. Add the bell pepper, celery, green onions, pimentos, chili sauce, Worcestershire sauce, Tabasco sauce and salt and mix well. Dissolve the gelatin in the lemon juice and water in the top of a double boiler, stirring to mix. Place over simmering water and heat for 5 to 10 minutes, stirring frequently. Fold into the cream cheese mixture. Add the shrimp and mix well. Pour into a chilled greased 2-quart gelatin mold. Refrigerate, covered, overnight. Unmold onto a serving platter and garnish as desired. Serve with crackers.

*Note:* You must start with 2 1/2 pounds of uncooked fresh shrimp, in order to produce the 6 cups of finely chopped cooked shrimp called for in this recipe.

*Yield: 30 to 40 servings*

# Shrimp Salsa Spread

8 ounces cream cheese, softened
2 1/2 cups cocktail sauce
1 1/2 cups (6 ounces) shredded mozzarella cheese
1 cup chopped green bell pepper
1 cup chopped tomato
1 cup chopped fresh mushrooms
3/4 cup sliced black olives
12 to 16 shrimp, cooked, peeled, sliced lengthwise

Spread the cream cheese over the bottom of a 9-inch dish. Pour the cocktail sauce evenly over the top. Sprinkle with the cheese. Layer with the bell pepper, tomato, mushrooms and olives. Top with the shrimp slices. Refrigerate, covered, until serving time. Serve with crackers.

*Note:* You may substitute lite cream cheese for the cream cheese if desired.

*Yield: 10 to 14 servings*

# Black Bean Salsa

1 (15-ounce) can black beans, rinsed, drained
1 (15-ounce) can Shoe Peg corn, drained
1 (15-ounce) can tomatoes with green chiles, drained
1 (4-ounce) can chopped green chiles
1 bunch green onions, chopped
4 teaspoons olive oil
Garlic salt to taste
Lemon pepper to taste
Cumin to taste
Basil to taste

Combine the black beans, corn, tomatoes with green chiles, undrained green chiles, green onions, olive oil, garlic salt, lemon pepper, cumin and basil in a bowl and mix well. Spoon into a serving dish. Serve at room temperature with corn chips. You may also heat the mixture and serve it warm as a vegetable side dish.

*Yield: (about) 4 cups salsa*

# Pico de Gallo

8 Roma tomatoes, chopped
1 large white onion, chopped
1 bunch fresh cilantro, chopped
5 serrano chiles, seeded, finely chopped
1/2 teaspoon salt

Combine the tomatoes, onion, cilantro, serrano chiles and salt in a bowl and mix well. Refrigerate, covered, until serving time. Serve with tortilla chips.

*Yield: (about) 4 cups relish*

# Marinated Lemon Olives

1 (6-ounce) can pitted large black olives
1 tablespoon olive oil
1/4 teaspoon grated lemon zest
1/2 teaspoon crushed red pepper flakes
1 garlic clove, minced
1/2 teaspoon freshly snipped thyme and/or oregano
1 lemon, thinly sliced

Combine the olives, olive oil, lemon zest, red pepper flakes, garlic, thyme and lemon slices in a bowl and mix well. Marinate, covered, in the refrigerator overnight.

*Yield: (about) 1 cup*

# Sweet Pickles

1 (1-quart) jar whole kosher pickles
2/3 cup sugar
2 heaping teaspoons celery seeds

Drain the pickles, discarding the liquid. Slice the pickles and return to the jar. Add the sugar and celery seeds and replace the lid. Shake the jar. Refrigerate for 3 days before serving.

*Yield: 1 quart*

# Bleu Cheese Pecan Grapes

4 ounces crumbled bleu cheese

3 ounces cream cheese, softened

4 ounces green seedless grapes, stems removed

1 cup finely chopped pecans or almonds, toasted

Combine the bleu cheese and cream cheese in a mixing bowl and beat until smooth. Refrigerate, covered, for 1 hour or longer. Wash the grapes and pat completely dry with paper towels. Wrap each grape with enough cheese mixture to completely cover. Roll in the pecans to coat. Refrigerate for 1 hour or longer.

*Yield: (about) 2 dozen*

# Spiced Mixed Nuts

1 egg white, lightly beaten

1 teaspoon water

1 2/3 cups dry-roasted peanuts

1/2 cup whole almonds

1/2 cup walnut halves

3/4 cup sugar

1 tablespoon pumpkin pie spice

3/4 teaspoon salt

Combine the egg white and water in a large bowl and whisk to blend. Add the peanuts, almonds and walnuts and toss to coat. Combine the sugar, pumpkin pie spice and salt in a small bowl and whisk to blend. Add to the nut mixture and toss until the nuts are well coated. Spread the mixture in a single layer on a lightly greased baking sheet. Bake at 300 degrees for 20 to 25 minutes, stirring halfway through the baking time. Cool on waxed paper. Break up any large clusters. Store in an airtight container.

*Yield: 4 1/2 cups*

Dining by Sunset

# Award-Winning Gumbo

1²/₃ pounds andouille sausage
4 ounces fresh garlic, chopped
6 ounces Jack Daniel's whiskey
1/3 bunch celery, chopped
2 red peppers, chopped
2 green peppers, chopped
1 onion, chopped
2 quarts clam juice
1/2 (6-ounce) can tomato filet
1/2 gallon water
21 ounces red wine
1/2 tablespoon dried oregano
1 teaspoon dried thyme
1 teaspoon cumin
1 teaspoon cayenne pepper
1 teaspoon black pepper
1/2 teaspoon white pepper
3 ounces Worcestershire sauce
1 1/2 ounces Durkee red hot sauce
1 1/2 ounces chicken base
1 ounce lobster base
1 ounce clam base
1 ounce shrimp base
2 pounds frozen okra, thawed
1 tablespoon gumbo filé
1 teaspoon salt

Render the sausage in a skillet until slightly brown. Add the garlic and brown slightly. Deglaze the skillet with the whiskey. Add the celery, peppers and onion and sauté lightly. Add the clam juice, tomato filet, water and red wine. Add the oregano, thyme, cumin, cayenne pepper, black pepper and white pepper. Stir in the Worcestershire sauce, hot sauce, chicken base, lobster base, clam base and shrimp base. Add a dark brown roux. Cook until desired thickness is achieved, but a minimum of 20 minutes to allow the roux to incorporate. Add the okra, gumbo filé and salt. Cool in metal pots.

*Yield: 2¹/₂ gallons*

*Sunset Bay Cafe at Sandestin*

# Creole Seafood Gumbo

2 pounds unpeeled large fresh shrimp

3 quarts water

1/2 cup shortening

1/2 cup flour

2 green bell peppers, chopped

4 ribs celery, chopped

2 large onions, chopped

1 pound crabmeat, shells removed, flaked

1/4 cup (1/2 stick) butter

2 tablespoons salt

2 teaspoons black pepper

1 tablespoon thyme

1/4 teaspoon cayenne pepper

4 bay leaves

3 tablespoons Worcestershire sauce

2 (16-ounce) cans diced tomatoes

2 (16-ounce) cans okra, finely chopped

Peel the shrimp, reserving the shells. Bring the water to a boil in a stockpot. Boil the shells for 1 hour. Drain and discard the shells, reserving the shrimp stock. Combine the shortening and flour in a glass measuring cup and cover with a paper towel. Microwave for 3 to 5 minutes or until the roux is the desired degree of darkness, stirring at 1-minute intervals and watching carefully to prevent burning. Spoon the roux into a stockpot. Add the bell peppers, celery and onions and cook until the moisture is reduced, stirring constantly.

Sauté the shrimp and crabmeat in the butter in a sauté pan. Add to the vegetable mixture. Add the salt, black pepper, thyme, cayenne pepper, bay leaves and Worcestershire sauce and mix well. Pour the reserved shrimp stock over the shrimp mixture and stir to mix. Add the tomatoes and bring the mixture to a boil, stirring constantly. Reduce the heat. Simmer for 2 to 2 1/2 hours, stirring occasionally. Add the okra and cook for 20 minutes longer or until the gumbo is thick. Remove and discard the bay leaves before serving.

*Yield: 12 main course servings, or 25 appetizer servings*

# Mexican Chicken Corn Soup

1 small onion, chopped
2 garlic cloves, minced
Butter for sautéing
5 boneless skinless chicken breasts, cooked, chopped
3 (15-ounce) cans chicken broth
1 (10-ounce) can tomatoes with green chiles
3 (15-ounce) cans cream-style corn
1 teaspoon hot red pepper sauce, or to taste
1 teaspoon cumin
Dash of salt
1/2 cup chopped fresh cilantro
2 cups (8 ounces) shredded Monterey Jack or Cheddar cheese

Sauté the onion and garlic in a small amount of butter in a stockpot until tender. Add the chicken, broth, tomatoes with green chiles, corn, hot red pepper sauce, cumin, salt, cilantro and cheese and mix well. Cook over low heat for 30 to 60 minutes, stirring frequently. Ladle into soup bowls and serve. You may omit the cheese from the soup and use half as much as a garnish.

*Yield: 10 to 12 servings*

## Memories

*Mary Lutz and her husband, Arno, report that bird watching at Sandestin is almost as exciting as other sporting activities on the resort. It is the first sport they undertook as a retired couple when they moved to Sandestin as full-time residents; golf came later. The bird population can be compared to the human population at Sandestin: full-time residents, snowbirds, and seasonal tourists. Mary is also the author of a recently published book about the Emerald Coast.*

# Corn and Crab Chowder

## CRAB CAKES

1 pound lump crabmeat, shells
   removed, flaked
4 ounces white bread crumbs
3 ounces mayonnaise
1/2 teaspoon dry mustard
1/4 cup dry sherry

3 fresh chives, snipped
1 teaspoon Old Bay seasoning
Salt and black pepper to taste
Cayenne pepper to taste
Clarified butter for sautéing

## CORN CHOWDER

12 ounces fresh corn kernels (cut from
   the cobs)
1 medium onion, chopped
1/2 cup finely chopped celery
1/2 cup finely chopped carrots
1/4 cup (1/2 stick) butter
2 ounces flour
6 cups chicken stock
1 cup white wine

2 large potatoes, peeled, finely
   chopped
1 bouquet garni
1/2 teaspoon basil
1/2 teaspoon thyme
1 teaspoon chopped fresh chives
1 cup heavy cream
Salt and pepper to taste

*For the crab cakes*, combine the crabmeat, bread crumbs, mayonnaise, dry mustard, wine, chives, Old Bay seasoning, salt, black pepper and cayenne pepper in a bowl and mix well. Divide and shape the mixture into 2-ounce crab cakes. Sauté the crab cakes in clarified butter in a skillet until cooked through and brown. Drain on paper towels and keep warm while preparing the chowder.

*For the chowder*, sauté the corn, onion, celery and carrots in the butter in a stockpot until the onion is translucent. Add the flour and cook for 10 minutes or until thickened, stirring constantly. Add the stock and wine gradually, stirring constantly until smooth. Add the potatoes, bouquet garni, basil, thyme and chives and mix well. Cook for 20 minutes, stirring frequently. Stir in the cream, salt and pepper. Remove and discard the bouquet garni.

*To serve*, ladle the chowder into soup bowls and top with 1 or 2 warm crab cakes.

*Yield: (about) 10 to 12 servings*

*Hilton Hotel's Sandcastles Restaurant*

# Cabbage Soup

3 slices flanken (beef short ribs), wide
   bones or soup bones
1 head cabbage, cut into quarters,
   sliced
1 fresh beet, chopped (optional)
1 (28-ounce) can tomatoes

1/2 cup ketchup
Juice of 1 lemon
1/2 cup sugar
Salt and pepper to taste
1/2 teaspoon crushed red pepper
   flakes

Combine the flanken, cabbage, beet, undrained tomatoes, ketchup, lemon juice, sugar, salt, pepper and red pepper flakes in a large stockpot and fill with water to cover. Bring to a boil, stirring frequently. Reduce the heat. Cook for 1 1/2 hours or until the flanken is tender. Remove the flanken using tongs and cut into squares, discarding any bones. Return the flanken to the soup and heat through. Ladle into soup bowls and serve. You may freeze this soup.

*Yield: (about) 6 servings*

# Santa Fe Soup

2 pounds ground beef or turkey
1 onion, chopped
2 envelopes ranch salad dressing mix
2 envelopes taco seasoning mix
1 (16-ounce) can black beans
1 (16-ounce) can kidney beans

1 (16-ounce) can pinto beans
1 (16-ounce) can tomatoes with green
   chiles
1 (16-ounce) can tomato wedges
2 (16-ounce) cans white corn
2 cups water

Brown the ground beef with the onion in a stockpot, stirring until the ground beef is crumbly; drain. Stir in the salad dressing mix and taco seasoning mix. Add the black beans, kidney beans, pinto beans, tomatoes with green chiles, tomato wedges, corn and water and mix well. Simmer for 2 hours, stirring occasionally and adding additional water if the soup is too thick. Ladle into soup bowls and garnish with sour cream, shredded Cheddar cheese and sliced green onions. Serve with tortilla chips. You may freeze this soup.

**Note:** Do not drain the beans, tomatoes or corn.

*Yield: 4 quarts*

# Vegetable Soup

1 pound ground round
1 medium onion, chopped
4 ribs celery, chopped
1 (10-ounce) can beef broth
1 (10-ounce) can French onion soup
1 (10-ounce) can potato soup
1/2 soup can of water

1 large tomato, peeled, chopped
1 (15-ounce) can tomato sauce
1 (28-ounce) package frozen mixed
  vegetables for soup, thawed
1 (15-ounce) can whole kernel corn
1 (15-ounce) can green beans

Brown the ground round with the onion and celery in a stockpot, stirring until the ground round is crumbly; drain. Add the broth, French onion soup, potato soup and water and mix well. Add the tomato, tomato sauce, mixed vegetables, undrained corn and undrained green beans and mix well. Bring to a boil, stirring frequently. Reduce the heat and simmer until heated through, stirring frequently. Ladle into soup bowls and serve.

*Yield: (about) 8 servings*

## Super Bowl Chili

1 pound ground beef
2 (15-ounce) cans chili beans
1 (15-ounce) can hot chili beans
1 (28-ounce) can diced tomatoes
1 large onion, chopped
1 green bell pepper, chopped
3 garlic cloves, chopped

3 tablespoons wine vinegar
3 tablespoons chili powder, or to taste
2 tablespoons sugar
1 tablespoon (or less) crushed red
  pepper flakes
1 teaspoon cumin
1 ounce unsweetened chocolate

Brown the ground beef in a skillet, stirring until the ground beef is crumbly; drain. Place the browned ground beef in a stockpot. Add the undrained beans, undrained tomatoes, onion, bell pepper, garlic, vinegar, chili powder, sugar, crushed red pepper flakes, cumin and chocolate and mix well. Simmer for 1 hour, stirring frequently. Ladle into chili bowls and serve.

*Yield: 6 servings*

## Portobello Mushroom Chili

5 cups chopped stemmed portobello
  mushrooms
3 cups water
1 cup coarsely chopped yellow onion
2 teaspoons chopped garlic

2 cups tomato sauce
1 tablespoon chili powder
1 teaspoon salt
1/2 teaspoon cumin
Pinch of cayenne pepper

Combine the mushrooms, water, onion, garlic, tomato sauce, chili powder, salt, cumin and cayenne pepper in a soup pot and mix well. Bring to a boil. Reduce the heat and simmer for 15 minutes, stirring frequently. Ladle into soup bowls and garnish with shredded Cheddar cheese and green onion slices.

*Yield: 6 servings*

# Vegetarian Chili

2 tablespoons vegetable oil

1 onion, chopped

2 carrots, thinly sliced

1 green bell pepper, coarsely chopped

2 small zucchini, cut into 1/2-inch pieces

2 small yellow squash, cut into 1/2-inch pieces

1 (28-ounce) can crushed tomatoes

2 (15-ounce) cans dark red kidney beans, rinsed, drained

1 (15-ounce) can whole kernel corn

1 (6-ounce) can tomato paste

1 (4-ounce) can chopped green chiles

6 tablespoons chili powder

1 tablespoon cumin

2 tablespoons sugar

1 to 2 teaspoons salt, or to taste

1/2 teaspoon pepper

Heat the oil in a large heavy pot over medium heat. Sauté the onion, carrots and bell pepper in the hot oil for 8 minutes. Add the zucchini and yellow squash and cook for 8 minutes longer or until all of the vegetables are tender, stirring frequently.

Add the tomatoes, kidney beans, undrained corn, tomato paste, undrained green chiles, chili powder, cumin, sugar, salt and pepper and mix well. Bring to a boil, stirring constantly. Reduce the heat. Simmer gently for 1 hour, stirring occasionally. Ladle into soup bowls and garnish with sour cream and shredded Cheddar cheese.

*Yield: 6 servings*

# Burnt Pine Steak au Poivre

4 (10- to 12-ounce) New York strip steaks, trimmed
Salt to taste
1 cup black peppercorns
1/2 cup olive oil
2 tablespoons olive oil
1/2 cup minced shallots
1 garlic clove, minced
1/4 cup brandy
1 cup demi-glace
1/4 cup heavy cream
1 tablespoon finely chopped fresh parsley

Season the steaks on both sides with salt. Grind the peppercorns coarsely in a coffee grinder. Rub 1/2 cup olive oil evenly over all sides of the steaks. Press 1/2 of the ground peppercorns into 1 side of each steak. Turn the steaks over. Press the remaining ground peppercorns into the other side of each steak.

Heat 2 tablespoons olive oil in a large skillet over medium heat. Sear the steaks in the hot oil for 4 to 5 minutes on each side. Remove the steaks to a platter. Sauté the shallots and garlic in the hot oil for 15 seconds. Remove from the heat. Add the brandy and carefully ignite the mixture.

Add the demi-glace and cream after the flames subside and mix well. Simmer for 1 minute. Add the steaks to the pan. Cook for 1 minute on each side. Place 1 steak on each of 4 serving plates. Stir the parsley into the sauce in the pan. Spoon some of the sauce over each steak. Serve with whipped potatoes and sautéed asparagus.

*Yield: 4 servings*

*Sunset Bay Cafe at Sandestin*

# Steak Diane

*This is adapted from a Julia Child recipe.*

4 (8-ounce) steaks such as top sirloin, Delmonico or rib-eye
Freshly ground pepper
Few drops of soy sauce
Few drops of olive oil or peanut oil
1 tablespoon cornstarch
1 tablespoon Dijon mustard
1 cup beef bouillon
1 tablespoon olive oil or peanut oil
1/4 cup (1/2 stick) butter
1/4 cup minced shallots
1/4 cup minced fresh parsley
Few drops of Worcestershire sauce
Juice of 1/2 lemon

Trim and discard the fat and gristle from the steaks. Pound the steaks 1 at a time between sheets of waxed paper to 1/4-inch thickness. Rub each steak with pepper, the soy sauce and a few drops of olive oil. Roll each steak as for a jelly roll starting from 1 short end. Arrange the rolls on a platter and refrigerate, covered, until serving time. Combine the cornstarch, Dijon mustard and bouillon in a bowl and whisk to blend.

Heat a skillet over medium heat. Pour in 1 tablespoon olive oil. Add 2 tablespoons of the butter and heat just until the butter begins to brown. Unroll 2 steaks into the skillet. Sauté for 30 to 40 seconds on each side. Reroll the steaks with a fork and return to the platter. Repeat the process with the 2 remaining steaks. Add the remaining butter to the skillet. Stir in the shallots and parsley and cook for 1 minute. Stir in the bouillon mixture. Add the Worcestershire sauce and lemon juice and stir to mix. Unroll each steak into the sauce to coat. Arrange the steaks on hot dinner plates and serve.

*Yield: 4 servings*

# Beef Burgundy Tenderloin

2 cups burgundy
1 cup olive oil
1 cup soy sauce
1 cup tarragon vinegar
2 tablespoons parsley flakes
2 tablespoons paprika
1 tablespoon Beau Monde seasoning
2 (3-pound) beef tenderloins

Combine the wine, olive oil, soy sauce, vinegar, parsley, paprika and Beau Monde seasoning in a bowl and whisk to blend. Pour into a 9×13-inch baking dish. Wipe the tenderloins gently with a dampened paper towel. Arrange the tenderloins in the marinade, turning to coat. Marinate, tightly covered, in the refrigerator for 2 hours, turning after 1 hour.

Uncover the dish and place on the bottom rack of the oven; do not drain the marinade. Broil for 15 minutes. Turn the tenderloins and broil for 15 minutes longer. Reduce the oven temperature to 350 degrees. Bake, covered, for 10 to 15 minutes or until a meat thermometer inserted in the thickest portion registers medium-rare or medium.

*Note:* The tenderloins will continue to cook slightly while resting before being carved, therefore cooking only to medium-rare is recommended.

*Yield: 8 servings*

## Memories

*Nancy and Cecil Oliver moved to Sandestin in 1981 from their cotton plantation in Arkansas. Nancy immediately became Sandestin's hostess, welcoming neighbors, newcomers, and "orphans" (the name for those without family in the area). Cecil was active in the community, serving for many years on the SOA Board and as president of Linkside Village Association, and, in fact, Lake Oliver is named for him.*

# Grilled London Broil

2/3 cup olive oil

1/3 cup lemon juice

1/3 cup wine vinegar

1/4 cup soy sauce

3 tablespoons Worcestershire sauce

1 onion, sliced, separated into rings

2 garlic cloves, minced

2 teaspoons dry mustard

3 to 4 tablespoons prepared mustard

1/2 teaspoon salt

1/2 teaspoon pepper

2 bay leaves

1 tablespoon parsley flakes

1/2 teaspoon ginger

1 (4-pound, 1 1/2- to 2-inch-thick) London broil, or sirloin steaks

Combine the olive oil, lemon juice, vinegar, soy sauce and Worcestershire sauce in a bowl and whisk to blend. Add the onion, garlic, dry mustard, prepared mustard, salt, pepper, bay leaves, parsley and ginger and mix well. Place the steak in a 2-gallon sealable plastic freezer bag. Pour the marinade over the steak and seal the bag. Marinate in the refrigerator overnight.

Remove the steak from the marinade, reserving the marinade. Grill the steak on a grill rack over hot coals to the desired degree of doneness. Remove to a platter and let stand. Remove the onion from the marinade; reserve the onion. Bring the reserved marinade to a boil in a 1-quart saucepan. Boil for 1 minute. Remove from the heat. Remove and discard the bay leaves. Return the onion to the marinade.

Slice the steak on the bias 1/8 to 1/4 inch thick. Arrange the slices on a serving platter and drizzle with the marinade. Serve with French or Italian bread.

*Yield: 6 servings*

# Never-Fail Roast Beef

1 well-marbleized standing rib roast
Salt and pepper to taste

Let the roast stand at room temperature for 1 hour. Season the roast with salt and pepper and place in a shallow roasting pan; do not add water. Roast, uncovered, at 375 degrees for 1 hour. Turn off the oven. Let stand in the oven with the oven door closed. Preheat the oven to 375 degrees 30 to 40 minutes before serving time. Roast for 30 to 40 minutes longer or until the meat is brown and crisp on the outside and medium-rare and juicy on the inside. Slice and serve. You may use any size roast for this recipe.

*Yield: variable*

# Beef Brisket

1 cup ketchup
1 cup chili sauce
1 envelope onion soup mix
1/2 (16-ounce) can whole cranberry sauce
1 (2 1/2- to 3-pound) beef brisket, fat trimmed
2 cups water

Combine the ketchup, chili sauce, onion soup mix and cranberry sauce in a bowl and mix well. Line a 13×15-inch roasting pan with extra-heavy-duty foil. Place a second sheet of foil large enough to wrap the brisket in the pan. Spoon 1/2 of the sauce onto the foil. Place the brisket on top. Spoon the remaining sauce over the brisket and wrap the foil tightly around the brisket and sauce. Pour the water into the foil-lined pan around the wrapped brisket. Bake at 350 degrees for 1 3/4 hours. Cool in the pan for 30 minutes. Slice the brisket against the grain and return to the sauce. Wrap and seal tightly in the foil. Bake for 45 minutes longer.

*3 hours total cook time*

*Yield: 4 to 6 servings*

# Slow-Cooker Steak

*This is good for a day at the beach. Dinner's almost ready when you return home.*

2 to 3 pounds beef round or sirloin steak, cut into serving-size pieces
1 (10-ounce) can cream of mushroom soup
1 soup can of water
1 envelope onion-mushroom soup mix
Hot cooked rice or noodles

Place the steak in a slow cooker. Add the cream of mushroom soup, water and onion-mushroom soup mix and stir to mix. Cook on Low for 8 to 10 hours or until done to taste. Serve over hot cooked rice or noodles.

*Yield: 6 to 8 servings*

# Shish Kabobs

### LEMON AND OREGANO MARINADE

1$\frac{1}{2}$ cups vegetable oil
1 cup fresh lemon juice
2 teaspoons salt
$\frac{1}{4}$ teaspoon freshly ground pepper
1 tablespoon chopped onion

1 garlic clove, minced, or $\frac{1}{4}$ teaspoon
  garlic powder
1 tablespoon oregano
$\frac{1}{2}$ teaspoon thyme
$\frac{1}{4}$ teaspoon rosemary

### SIRLOIN SHISH KABOBS

12 small onions, ends trimmed
2 pounds top sirloin steak, cut into
   1-inch cubes
2 large green bell peppers, rinsed,
   cut into halves lengthwise, seeded

12 medium mushrooms, cleaned,
   stems removed
12 cherry tomatoes, rinsed, stems
   removed
12 lemon slices (2 lemons)

*For the marinade,* combine the oil, lemon juice, salt, pepper, onion, garlic, oregano, thyme and rosemary in a bowl and whisk to blend.

*For the shish kabobs,* drop the unpeeled onions into a pot of boiling water. Parboil for 5 to 8 minutes. Remove with a slotted spoon. Arrange the steak cubes in the bottom of a large roasting pan. Pour the marinade over the steak. Cut each bell pepper half into thirds lengthwise. Add the bell peppers and mushrooms to the marinating steak. Refrigerate, covered, for 3 hours or longer. Refrigerate the tomatoes, covered, separately.

Assemble the kabobs 30 minutes before serving time. Thread each of 6 skewers with 4 steak cubes, 2 lemon slices, 2 onions, 2 bell pepper strips, 2 mushroom caps and 2 cherry tomatoes $\frac{1}{2}$ at a time in any attractive order. Discard any remaining marinade. Arrange the kabobs on a foil-lined tray to catch any marinade drips. Refrigerate, covered, until ready to grill. Arrange the kabobs on a grill rack 4 inches above low-burning coals. Grill 10 minutes or longer (depending on the temperature of the fire) to the desired degree of doneness, turning at least once. You may broil the kabobs 4 inches from the heat source in the oven for 10 minutes, turning once.

*Yield: 6 servings*

# Venison Scallopini

*Venison (deer meat) is exceptionally healthy—no fat and no preservatives!*

1 pound venison loin steaks
Flour for coating
1 orange or yellow bell pepper, chopped
1 onion, chopped
Sliced mushrooms to taste
Vegetable oil for browning
Hot cooked rice

Pound the steaks between sheets of plastic wrap into scallopini. Coat the scallopini lightly on each side with flour. Grease or spray a skillet with nonstick cooking spray. Heat over medium-high heat. Sauté the bell pepper, onion and mushrooms in the prepared pan until tender. Remove from the heat. Brown the scallopini in a small amount of oil in a separate skillet for 5 minutes, turning once. Spoon hot cooked rice onto a serving platter. Top with the onion mixture and the scallopini.

*Yield: 4 servings*

## Entertaining Hints

*For your next cookout, follow these simple tips. Always preheat the grill or burn the charcoal down to glowing coals. A grill brush is a must; use a long-handled stiff wire brush for cleaning grill racks. Use a spatula or tongs to place food on the grill. Take care not to pierce the food with a fork, or the natural juices will run out, leaving your food dry. Resist the temptation to move the food a lot on the grill; try to turn food over only once or twice. Use a timer so you do not overcook your dinner. And last, be sure to eat grilled foods while they are hot. Grilling cooks food; it does not preserve it.*

# Chicken Piccata

4 boneless skinless chicken breasts
1 1/2 cups fresh bread crumbs
   (about 3 slices white bread)
1/2 teaspoon salt
1 egg
1 tablespoon milk
1/4 cup (1/2 stick) butter or margarine

1/2 cup water
1/4 cup dry white wine
1 chicken bouillon cube
Juice of 1 large lemon, or
   1 tablespoon concentrated
   lemon juice

Pound each chicken breast between sheets of plastic wrap into a 1/4-inch-thick cutlet. Combine the bread crumbs and salt in a shallow dish and mix well. Beat the egg with the milk in a shallow dish with a fork until well blended. Dip the chicken pieces into the egg mixture. Roll in the bread crumb mixture to coat both sides. Heat the butter in a skillet over medium heat. Cook the chicken in the hot butter for 5 minutes, turning once and adding additional butter if necessary. Remove the chicken to a platter; keep warm. Add the water, wine, bouillon cube and lemon juice to the drippings in the skillet and mix well. Bring to a boil over high heat, stirring constantly. Reduce the heat to low. Simmer, covered, for 5 minutes, stirring occasionally. Spoon the sauce over the chicken and serve.

*Yield: 4 servings*

# Chicken Louise

4 to 6 chicken breasts
1 teaspoon salt
1/4 teaspoon garlic salt or garlic
   powder
Dash of pepper
2 medium onions, sliced
8 ounces fresh mushrooms, sliced

1 cup water
1 (12-ounce) jar chili sauce
1/2 cup packed brown sugar
1 teaspoon Worcestershire sauce
1/2 cup sherry
1 (16-ounce) can pitted dark Bing
   cherries, drained

Arrange the chicken in a baking dish. Sprinkle with the salt, garlic salt and pepper. Layer with the onions and mushrooms. Bake at 350 degrees for 10 to 15 minutes. Combine the water, chili sauce, brown sugar and Worcestershire sauce in a bowl and mix well. Pour over the chicken. Bake, covered, for 45 minutes. Add the sherry and cherries. Bake, uncovered, for 15 minutes longer or until brown.

*Note:* For boneless skinless chicken breasts, reduce the baking time by half to two-thirds.

*Yield: 4 to 6 servings*

# Sesame Chicken

1 cup baking mix or flour
1 tablespoon poultry seasoning
1 tablespoon seasoned salt
2 tablespoons sesame seeds
1/2 cup finely chopped pecans
1 cup milk
1/2 cup (1 stick) butter, melted
4 to 6 boneless skinless chicken breasts

Combine the baking mix, poultry seasoning, seasoned salt, sesame seeds and pecans in a bowl and mix well. Pour the milk into a shallow bowl. Pour the melted butter into a shallow bowl. Dip each chicken breast in the milk and roll in the dry mixture to coat. Dip into the butter and arrange in a greased baking dish. Sprinkle with any remaining dry mixture and drizzle with any remaining butter. Bake at 350 degrees for 35 to 45 minutes or until cooked through.

*Yield: 4 to 6 servings*

# Kedjenou Chicken

2 to 3 fresh tomatoes, chopped, or 1 large can diced tomatoes
2 to 3 onions, chopped
1 or 2 garlic cloves, minced
1 medium eggplant, cut into 1-inch cubes
8 ounces fresh mushrooms, cut into halves
1 chicken, cut into quarters or eighths
Salt to taste
1 jalapeño chile, seeded, sliced
Hot cooked rice

Place the tomatoes in the bottom of a Dutch oven. Layer with the onions, garlic, eggplant and mushrooms. Top with the chicken pieces. Sprinkle with salt and jalapeño chile slices. Bake, covered, at 350 degrees for 45 to 60 minutes, shaking the pot every 10 minutes to keep the chicken from sticking to the pot. Serve over hot cooked rice.

*Note:* You may cook the chicken in the Dutch oven on the stovetop using the same temperature and cooking time.

*Yield: 4 to 8 servings*

# Chicken and Sausage

*This is guaranteed to tickle your taste buds!*

Vegetable oil for browning
12 boneless skinless chicken breasts
12 links sweet Italian sausage, casings removed
1/2 cup chicken broth
1 cup white wine
1 garlic clove, minced
1 large green bell pepper, sliced
1 cup chopped onion
1 cup sliced mushrooms
4 cups drained canned Italian plum tomatoes
1 (15-ounce) can tomato sauce
1 teaspoon sugar
1 teaspoon oregano
Hot cooked angel hair pasta or rice

Heat 1/4 inch of vegetable oil in a large sauté pan. Brown the chicken in the hot oil on both sides. Remove to a warm plate. Cut the sausage into serving-size pieces and add to the pan. Brown the sausage on all sides in the hot oil. Remove to the plate with the chicken.

Add the broth, wine, garlic, bell pepper, onion and mushrooms to the pan and stir to mix. Add the tomatoes, tomato sauce, sugar and oregano and mix well. Simmer for 15 minutes, stirring occasionally and scraping the browned bits from the bottom of the pan. Return the sausage and chicken to the pan. Simmer for 45 minutes. Serve over hot cooked angel hair pasta.

*Note:* You may prepare this in advance for a dinner party.

*Yield: 6 to 8 servings*

# Elegant Chicken and Shrimp

1/4 cup (1/2 stick) butter
2 medium garlic cloves, minced
8 boneless skinless chicken breasts
8 ounces fresh mushrooms, cut into
   thick slices
2 (10-ounce) cans cream of
   chicken soup

1/2 cup half-and-half
1/4 cup grated Parmesan cheese
1 pound deveined peeled fresh shrimp
6 cups hot cooked rice
1/2 cup (1 stick) butter, melted
1/4 cup chopped fresh watercress

Melt 1/4 cup butter in a large skillet. Cook the garlic in the butter for 2 minutes. Brown the chicken on both sides in the garlic butter. Add the mushrooms and sauté for 1 minute. Stir in the soup, half-and-half, cheese and shrimp. Cook, covered, over low heat until the chicken is cooked through and the shrimp turn pink, stirring occasionally. Combine the rice, 1/2 cup melted butter and the watercress in a bowl and stir to mix. Serve the chicken mixture over the rice.

*Note:* Fat-free half-and-half may be substituted for the half-and-half.

*Yield: 6 to 8 servings*

# Chicken and Dressing Casserole

1 chicken, boiled, drained
4 cups crumbled corn bread
1/2 cup (1 stick) margarine, melted
1 cup chicken broth
1/2 cup chopped onion
1/2 cup chopped celery
1/4 cup chopped green onions

1/2 cup mayonnaise
1/2 teaspoon salt
2 eggs
Milk
1 to 2 (10-ounce) cans cream of
   mushroom soup
1/4 cup grated Parmesan cheese

Chop the boiled chicken, discarding the skin and bones; set aside. Combine the corn bread, margarine and broth in a bowl and mix well. Spoon 1/2 of the corn bread mixture into a 9x13-inch baking dish. Combine the chicken, onion, celery, green onions, mayonnaise and salt in a bowl and mix well. Spread over the prepared layer in the baking dish. Top with the remaining corn bread mixture. Beat the eggs in a 1-cup measuring cup. Add enough milk to measure 1 cup. Pour over the prepared layers. Refrigerate, covered with plastic wrap, overnight. Unwrap and spread the soup over the layers. Bake at 350 degrees for 30 to 40 minutes. Sprinkle with the cheese. Bake for 10 minutes longer.

*Yield: 6 to 8 servings*

# Chicken Divan

4 chicken breasts
4 cups water
3 bay leaves
2 garlic cloves
1 onion, cut into quarters
2 carrots, cut into halves
1 rib celery, cut into halves
1 teaspoon parsley flakes
1/2 teaspoon pepper

1 bunch fresh broccoli, trimmed
1 (10-ounce) can cream of chicken
   soup
1/2 cup mayonnaise
1/2 teaspoon salt
1/2 teaspoon curry powder
1 cup (4 ounces) shredded Cheddar
   cheese
Cracker or crouton crumbs to taste

Place the chicken in a stockpot with the water, bay leaves, garlic, onion, carrots, celery, parsley and pepper. Bring to a boil. Reduce the heat. Simmer for 30 to 45 minutes or until the chicken is cooked through. Remove the chicken to a platter to cool.

Strain the stock, reserving it for another use and discarding the solids. Cut the broccoli into bite-size pieces and steam until tender-crisp. You may microwave the broccoli in a microwave-safe container on High for 5 to 7 minutes or until tender-crisp. Cut the chicken into bite-size pieces, discarding the skin and bones.

Place the broccoli in a buttered baking dish. Top with the chicken. Combine the soup, mayonnaise, salt and curry powder in a bowl and mix well. Pour over the chicken. Sprinkle evenly with the cheese and cracker crumbs. Bake at 350 degrees until the cheese is melted.

*Yield: 4 to 6 servings*

# White Lasagna

6 chicken breasts

1 1/4 cups chicken broth

1 cup water

1 tablespoon salt

3/4 cup (1 1/2 sticks) butter

7 1/2 tablespoons flour

2 cups milk

1 1/2 cups heavy cream

1/2 teaspoon rosemary

1/2 teaspoon tarragon

1/2 teaspoon salt

1/2 teaspoon celery salt

1 teaspoon nutmeg

1 1/2 cups grated Parmesan cheese

3 quarts water

1/4 cup vegetable oil

8 ounces lasagna noodles

8 ounces sliced deli ham

Chopped celery to taste

Combine the chicken, broth, 1 cup water and 1 tablespoon salt in a stockpot. Bring to a boil. Reduce the heat. Simmer until the chicken is cooked through. Remove from the heat. Let stand for 30 minutes. Drain the chicken, reserving 1 cup of the cooking liquid.

Melt the butter in a large saucepan. Blend in the flour. Cook over medium heat until the mixture begins to boil and thicken, stirring constantly. Add the milk, cream and reserved cooking liquid and mix well. Cook until thickened, stirring constantly. Add the rosemary, tarragon, 1/2 teaspoon salt, the celery salt and nutmeg and mix well. Remove from the heat. Stir in the cheese. Chop the chicken into small pieces, discarding the skin and bones.

Bring 3 quarts water and the oil to a boil in a stockpot. Cook the lasagna noodles in the boiling water mixture using the package directions. Drain on paper towels.

Layer the lasagna noodles, cheese sauce, chicken, ham and celery 1/2 at a time in a buttered 9×13-inch baking dish. Bake at 350 degrees for 25 to 35 minutes. Garnish with parsley.

*Yield: 8 to 10 servings*

# Cajun Duck with Creole Sauce

## CAJUN DUCK

1 (1¹/₂- to 2-pound) duck
1 tablespoon salt
1 tablespoon pepper
¹/₄ cup vegetable oil

1 medium onion, sliced
6 garlic cloves, cut into halves
1 cup chicken stock

## CREOLE SAUCE

2 tablespoons flour
2 tablespoons vegetable oil
¹/₄ cup vegetable oil
1 cup peeled crawfish tails

1 cup peeled fresh shrimp
1 cup minced garlic
¹/₄ cup chopped onion
2 cups seafood stock

**For the duck,** split the duck in half. Rub the duck all over with the salt and pepper. Heat the oil in a Dutch oven. Add the duck, onion and garlic. Sear the duck for 3 minutes on each side until brown. Add the stock. Simmer for 25 minutes. Remove the duck to a steel oven plate or broiler pan. Discard the onion and garlic. Broil the duck for 3¹/₂ minutes on each side until crisp. Remove to a warm platter.

**For the sauce,** combine the flour and 2 tablespoons oil in a small saucepan and mix well. Cook over medium heat until the roux darkens and thickens, stirring constantly. Remove from the heat. Heat ¹/₄ cup oil in a saucepan over high heat. Add the crawfish tails, shrimp, garlic and onion and cook for 2 minutes, stirring constantly. Stir in the stock. Cook for 5 minutes, stirring frequently. Reduce the heat to medium and add the roux. Cook until the mixture thickens, stirring constantly. Spoon the Creole Sauce over the duck halves and serve.

*Yield: 2 servings*

Poppy's Seafood Factory

# Sherried Quail

*This recipe should appeal to the hunters in the area.*

1 cup flour
Salt and pepper to taste
2 (10-ounce) cans (or more) cream of chicken soup
¼ cup (½ stick) butter or margarine
4 quail
½ cup cooking sherry

Combine the flour, salt and pepper in a bowl and mix well. Heat the soup in a large saucepan until bubbly; keep warm. Melt the butter in a skillet. Dip each quail in the flour mixture to coat. Brown the quail quickly on all sides in the hot butter. Add half the wine to the soup and stir to mix. Add the quail to the soup, adding additional soup, if necessary, to completely immerse the quail. Bring to a boil slowly. Reduce the heat. Simmer, covered, for 3 hours. Stir in the remaining wine. Place the quail in a deep serving dish and top with the gravy.

*Yield: 2 to 3 servings*

# Pork Tenderloin

*This is a unique dish for special company because the preparation is quite simple, yet the presentation is delightfully spectacular. Serve with a dry California rosé.*

## MUSTARD SAUCE

1/3 cup sour cream
1/3 cup mayonnaise
1 tablespoon dry mustard
1 tablespoon finely chopped
   green onions

1 1/2 teaspoons wine vinegar
Salt and pepper to taste

## PORK TENDERLOIN

1 (2 1/2- to 3-pound) pork tenderloin
2 tablespoons brown sugar

1/4 cup soy sauce

**For the sauce,** combine the sour cream, mayonnaise, dry mustard, green onions, vinegar, salt and pepper in a bowl and whisk to blend. Refrigerate, covered, overnight for best flavor. Bring to room temperature before serving.

**For the tenderloin,** place the pork in a glass dish. Mix the brown sugar and soy sauce in a small bowl. Pour over the pork. Turn the pork to coat all sides. Refrigerate, covered, for several hours. Bring the pork to room temperature. Arrange on a rack in a shallow roasting pan. Bake at 300 degrees for 2 hours, basting frequently with the marinade. Do not baste during the last 15 minutes of roasting time. Let the pork stand for 10 minutes before slicing. Serve with the Mustard Sauce spooned over the top. Serve with asparagus and lemon-laced apples and yams on the side.

**Note:** It is safe to baste the pork tenderloin with the uncooked marinade as long as there is additional roasting time left. Do not baste during the last 15 minutes of roasting time and do not baste after the tenderloin is removed from the oven unless the marinade is boiled in a saucepan.

*Yield: 4 to 6 servings*

# Black-Tie Pork Tenderloin

4 pounds pork tenderloin
Flour for coating
Vegetable oil for browning
2 tablespoons butter, softened
1 3/4 cups currant jelly
1 1/2 teaspoons salt

1/2 teaspoon pepper
2 teaspoons rosemary
1 1/3 tablespoons flour
1 1/3 cups whipping cream
Hot cooked rice

Roll the pork in flour to lightly coat. Heat a small amount of oil in a roasting pan set over two burners. Brown the pork slowly in the hot oil. Spread the pork evenly with the butter and jelly. Sprinkle evenly with the salt, pepper and rosemary. Bake, covered, at 350 degrees until a meat thermometer inserted in the thickest portion registers 165 degrees. Remove the pork from the pan and keep warm on a platter. Blend 1 1/3 tablespoons flour and the cream in a bowl. Add to the drippings in the roasting pan, stirring to blend. Return the pork to the pan. Bake, covered, for 15 minutes longer. Let stand for 10 minutes before slicing. Serve over hot cooked rice.

*Yield: 8 to 10 servings*

# Grilled Tenderloin

1/4 cup (1/2 stick) butter, softened
1 tablespoon molasses
1/2 teaspoon fresh lemon juice
4 (1 1/2-inch-thick) boneless center-cut pork loin chops
1/4 cup coarsely ground pepper
Salt to taste

Combine the butter, molasses and lemon juice in a bowl and mix well. Refrigerate, covered, until serving time. Rub the loin chops on both sides with the pepper. Arrange on a grill rack over medium coals. Grill for 12 to 15 minutes. Turn the loin chops and grill until cooked through. Arrange on a serving platter and top each loin chop with the molasses butter. Season with salt.

*Yield: 4 servings*

# Santa Fe Pork Chops

**FIRECRACKER SALSA**

1 (20-ounce) can pineapple tidbits,
  drained
1 medium cucumber, chopped

1 tablespoon brown sugar
1 jalapeño chile, minced

**SEASONED PORK CHOPS**

1 tablespoon chili powder
1 tablespoon cumin
1 tablespoon pepper

1/2 teaspoon salt
6 (11/2-inch) pork chops

*For the salsa*, combine the pineapple, cucumber, brown sugar and jalapeño chile in a bowl and mix well. Refrigerate, covered, for 4 to 24 hours.

*For the pork chops,* combine the chili powder, cumin, pepper and salt in a bowl and mix well. Coat each pork chop on both sides with the seasoning mixture. Place the pork chops in a sealable plastic bag and seal the bag. Refrigerate for 1 to 2 hours. Arrange the pork chops on a grill rack over medium coals. Grill for 7 to 8 minutes. Turn the chops and grill for 7 minutes longer or until cooked through. Serve with the salsa on the side.

*Yield: 6 servings*

## Local Interest

*Spanish explorers first dropped anchor in the waters of what is now called Choctawhatchee Bay back in the 16th century. The Spanish were convinced this new world offered riches in gold and other precious minerals. Other colorful characters figured in the history of the Emerald Coast, including a number of pirates who built their wealth plundering cargo ships. Over the years, stories of sunken ships and hidden treasure continue to capture the imagination of young and old alike. The most popular story is that of Billy Bowlegs. According to legend, the infamous pirate lost a ship laden with treasure in Choctawhatchee Bay near Sandestin. Reportedly, a federal cutter ship fired upon the pirate's ship. It sank and neither ship nor treasure was ever found. Who knows what booty lies beneath the sands of Sandestin!*

# Slow-Cooker Ribs

*The liquid smoke in this recipe imparts a wonderful hickory-smoked flavor as though you had smoked the ribs all day.*

1 or 2 lemons, cut into halves
3½ pounds pork loin back ribs or any style pork ribs
¼ cup packed brown sugar
1 teaspoon salt
½ teaspoon pepper
3 tablespoons liquid smoke
2 garlic cloves, finely chopped
1 medium onion, sliced
½ cup cola
1½ cups barbecue sauce

Squeeze the lemon halves over the pork ribs. Combine the brown sugar, salt, pepper, liquid smoke and garlic in a bowl and mix well. Rub into the pork ribs on both sides. Cut the pork ribs into 4-inch pieces. Spray the inside of a slow cooker with nonstick cooking spray. Layer the pork ribs and onion slices ½ at a time in the slow cooker. Pour the cola over the top. Cook, covered, on Low for 8 to 9 hours or until cooked through. Remove the pork ribs to a platter and spread with barbecue sauce. You may serve the ribs at this point or grill the ribs over medium coals for 15 minutes to give the ribs a stronger charcoal-smoked flavor.

*Note:* The cola adds a wonderful sweetness to the ribs, but if you don't have cola on hand, you may use water instead.

*Yield: 6 servings*

# Catfish Parmesan

*Flavorful and crispy, this recipe is a great alternative to fried catfish and produces impressive results without a lot of work.*

2/3 cup freshly grated Parmesan cheese
1/4 cup flour
1/2 teaspoon salt
1/4 teaspoon pepper
1 teaspoon paprika
1 egg, beaten
1/4 cup milk
2 pounds catfish fillets
1/4 cup (1/2 stick) butter, melted
1/3 cup sliced almonds

Combine the cheese, flour, salt, pepper and paprika in a bowl and mix well. Combine the egg and milk in a bowl and whisk to blend. Dip each catfish fillet in the egg mixture and then in the cheese mixture to coat all sides. Arrange in a single layer on a greased baking sheet. Drizzle with the butter and sprinkle with the almonds. Bake at 350 degrees for 35 to 40 minutes.

*Yield: 4 servings*

# Sautéed Flounder with Crawfish Cream Sauce

*This recipe won first prize in the seafood category of a contest run by a Lafayette, Louisiana, newspaper in the early 1980s.*

## CRAWFISH CREAM SAUCE

1 pound peeled crawfish
1/2 cup (1 stick) butter
1/2 bell pepper, finely chopped
1 egg yolk
1 cup half-and-half
1 bunch green onions, thinly sliced
6 garlic cloves, finely chopped
1 cup finely chopped fresh parsley

1/4 cup dry sherry
1/4 teaspoon each thyme, basil, oregano, salt and onion powder
1/2 teaspoon coarsely ground black pepper
1/2 teaspoon white pepper
1/8 teaspoon garlic powder

## SAUTÉED FLOUNDER

1/4 teaspoon salt
1/2 teaspoon coarsely ground black pepper
1/2 teaspoon white pepper
1/4 teaspoon onion powder

1/8 teaspoon garlic powder
1 pound flounder fillets (snapper and redfish are also acceptable)
1/2 cup flour
1/2 cup (1 stick) butter

**For the sauce,** rinse the crawfish to remove any fat. Sauté the crawfish in the butter in a heavy skillet over medium heat, adding the bell pepper while sautéing. Beat the egg yolk with the half-and-half in a bowl until smooth. Add to the crawfish mixture and mix well. Reduce the heat to low. Stir in the green onions, garlic, parsley, wine, thyme, basil, oregano, salt, onion powder, black pepper, white pepper and garlic powder. Cook over low heat for 5 minutes, stirring frequently; set aside.

**For the flounder,** combine the salt, black pepper, white pepper, onion powder and garlic powder in a bowl and mix well. Sprinkle evenly over the flounder fillets on both sides. Coat the flounder with the flour, shaking off any excess. Sauté the flounder in the butter in a skillet over medium-high heat until brown on both sides. Arrange the flounder on a serving platter and spoon the sauce over the top.

*Yield: 2 to 4 servings*

# Stuffed Flounder

1 (1-pound) flounder fillet
1/2 cup chopped peeled fresh shrimp
1/4 cup chopped celery
1/4 cup chopped bell pepper
1/4 cup chopped onion
Chopped fresh garlic to taste
1/2 teaspoon salt
1/2 teaspoon pepper
Juice of 1/2 lemon
1 cup claw crabmeat
1/2 cup bread crumbs
1/4 cup chopped fresh parsley
1 egg

Cut the flounder to create a pocket for stuffing. Sauté the shrimp, celery, bell pepper, onion, garlic, salt, pepper and lemon juice in a nonstick skillet until the onion is tender. Remove from the heat. Add the crabmeat, bread crumbs, parsley and egg and mix well. Stuff the crabmeat mixture into the flounder pocket, mounding the mixture as high as possible. Steam the stuffed flounder in a steamer for 5 minutes. Place on a broiler pan. Broil for 7 minutes. Garnish with lemon wedges.

*Yield: 4 to 6 servings*

 *Poppy's Seafood Factory*

## Memories

*One memorable Sandestin owner was Mary McCool. When Mary first moved to Sandestin from her home state of Arkansas, she became well-known for playing a mean game of tennis. She was also passionate about deep sea fishing. Mary and her son Wayne were also well-known for their simple but fun fish fries. Mary's favorite quip, which she cited often, was, "There are two kinds of people in the world. People who live in Sandestin and people who wish they did!"*

# Grouper Elizabeth

### ELEPHANT WALK BUTTER SAUCE

Zest and juice of 2 oranges
Zest and juice of 1 lemon
Zest and juice of 1 lime
1 head fennel, julienned
2 shallots, julienned
1 bay leaf

3 peppercorns
1/2 cup white wine
2 cups cream
4 cups (8 sticks) unsalted butter,
  softened

### GROUPER

4 (8-ounce) grouper fillets
Salt and pepper to taste

2 teaspoons clarified butter
1/4 cup white wine or butter stock

### CRABMEAT TOPPING

12 ounces Elephant Walk Butter Sauce
1/4 cup chopped fresh chives
1/2 cup chopped peeled tomatoes (1/2-inch pieces)
8 ounces jumbo lump crabmeat, shells removed, flaked

### GARNISH

1/4 cup sliced almonds, toasted

*For the butter sauce*, combine the orange zest, orange juice, lemon zest, lemon juice, lime zest, lime juice, fennel, shallots, bay leaf, peppercorns and white wine in a large skillet. Cook until reduced by 1/2, stirring constantly. Stir in the cream. Cook until reduced by half, stirring constantly. Add the butter a small amount at a time, stirring until smooth. Discard the bay leaf and peppercorns.

*For the grouper*, season the grouper on both sides with salt and pepper. Heat the clarified butter in a large ovenproof sauté pan to the smoking point. Cook the grouper skin side up in the hot butter until golden brown. Turn the grouper over and deglaze the pan with the wine, stirring to loosen any browned bits from the bottom of the pan. Bake at 400 degrees for 20 minutes.

*For the crabmeat topping*, heat the butter sauce in a saucepan. Add the chives, tomatoes and crabmeat and mix well. Cook until the crabmeat is cooked through.

*To serve*, arrange the grouper on a serving platter and top with the crabmeat topping. Garnish with the almonds.

*Yield: 4 servings*

*Elephant Walk at Sandestin*

# Grouper Floridian

## LEMON BUTTER SAUCE

1 cup white wine
1/4 cup lemon juice
1 garlic clove, minced

2 shallots, minced
2 cups heavy cream
1 cup (2 sticks) butter, softened

## MANGO RELISH

3 cups finely chopped mangoes
1 cup finely chopped pineapple
1 cup finely chopped papaya
1/4 cup finely chopped red bell pepper

1/4 cup finely chopped green onions
1/2 cup honey
2 tablespoons red wine vinegar

## SEARED GROUPER

1 cup olive oil

4 (6- to 8-ounce) grouper fillets

*For the sauce*, combine the wine, lemon juice, garlic and shallots in a saucepan over medium heat and mix well. Cook until the mixture is reduced by 90 percent, stirring occasionally. Stir in the cream. Cook until the mixture is reduced by 80 percent, or until the desired consistency is achieved. Remove from the heat. Whisk the butter into the sauce gradually. Stir until the sauce reaches the desired consistency.

*For the relish*, combine the mangoes, pineapple, papaya, bell pepper, green onions, honey and vinegar in a bowl and mix gently to coat. Refrigerate, covered, until serving time.

*For the grouper*, heat the olive oil in an ovenproof sauté pan over high heat until the olive oil begins to turn white. Sear the grouper fillets in the hot oil on 1 side until golden brown. Turn the grouper over and place the pan in the oven. Bake at 350 degrees for 8 to 12 minutes or until done.

*To serve*, arrange 1 fillet in the center of a plate. Place 2 tablespoons of the relish next to the grouper and lace the plate lightly with the sauce. Repeat with the remaining ingredients. Serve with a colorful vegetable medley and a starch of choice.

*Yield: 4 servings*

*Beach Club at Sandestin*

# Fried Mackerel

1 cup milk
3 tablespoons prepared mustard
Salt and pepper to taste
2 pounds fresh mackerel fillets, cut into 2-inch cubes
Seasoned fish fry coating (Zatarain's is recommended)
Peanut oil for deep-frying

Combine the milk, prepared mustard, salt and pepper in a sealable plastic bag. Add the mackerel and seal the bag. Knead the bag to mix. Marinate in the refrigerator for 2 hours or longer. Drain the mackerel, discarding the marinade. Place the fish fry coating in a paper bag. Add the mackerel and shake to coat. Fry in hot peanut oil in a skillet until golden brown. Remove with a slotted spoon to paper towels to drain. Serve with tartar sauce.

*Yield: 4 to 6 servings*

# Pecan-Encrusted Salmon

*Those who think they don't care for salmon should try this delicious recipe!*

| | |
|---|---|
| ¼ cup pecan halves | 1 pound salmon fillets |
| 1½ tablespoons honey | 1 tablespoon olive oil |
| 1½ tablespoons lemon juice | Garlic powder to taste |
| Red pepper flakes to taste | Salt and pepper to taste |

Scatter the pecans on a baking sheet. Bake at 350 degrees for 10 minutes or until toasted, shaking the baking sheet occasionally. Chop the pecans. Combine the pecans, honey, lemon juice and red pepper flakes in a bowl and mix well. Brush the flesh side of the salmon with the olive oil and sprinkle with the garlic powder, salt and pepper. Arrange the salmon on a grill rack skin side up over hot coals. Grill for 5 minutes. Turn the salmon over carefully and spoon the pecan mixture evenly over the top. Close the grill lid. Grill for 7 minutes longer.

*Yield: 4 servings*

# Salmon Pie

*A simple salmon recipe all the way from Sydney, Australia.*

| | |
|---|---|
| 1 cup uncooked rice | Grated nutmeg to taste |
| 1 (15-ounce) can red sockeye salmon | Salt and pepper to taste |
| 1 small onion, grated | 2 eggs, beaten |
| Chopped parsley to taste | Butter to taste |
| Lemon juice to taste | Grated Parmesan cheese to taste |

Cook the rice using the package directions. Drain the salmon, reserving the liquid. Remove and discard any bones from the salmon. Combine the rice, salmon and reserved liquid in a bowl and mix well. Add the onion, parsley, lemon juice, nutmeg, salt and pepper and mix well. Add the eggs and mix well. Spoon into a well-buttered glass pie plate. Dot the top with butter and sprinkle evenly with cheese. Bake at 350 degrees for 15 minutes.

*Note:* For Salmon Soufflé, substitute 3 eggs for the 2 eggs, adding the yolks first with a little milk. Fold in 3 stiffly beaten egg whites and bake the mixture in a soufflé dish.

*Yield: 6 servings*

# Pineapple Ginger Swordfish Steaks

1 (8-ounce) can crushed pineapple
1/4 cup chopped green onions with tops
2 tablespoons lime juice
1 tablespoon vegetable oil
1 tablespoon honey
1 teaspoon ginger
1 teaspoon salt
1 1/2 pounds (3/4- to 1-inch-thick) swordfish steaks

Bring the undrained pineapple, green onions, lime juice, oil, honey, ginger and salt to a boil in a saucepan over medium heat, stirring occasionally. Reduce the heat. Simmer, uncovered, for 3 minutes. Remove from the heat. Arrange the swordfish on a grill rack set 4 inches over medium coals. Close the grill lid. Grill for 10 to 15 minutes or until the fish flakes easily with a fork, turning once and brushing occasionally with the pineapple mixture. Cut into serving pieces. Serve with any remaining pineapple mixture. Garnish with sliced pineapple and green onions.

*Yield: 2 servings*

# Trout Amandine

*Choctawhatchee Bay is full of delicious fish. After a day of fishing in the bay aboard the Lil' Lucky with Captain Doug Richards, try this recipe for your catch of spotted sea trout, redfish, or black snapper.*

4 (4- to 8-ounce) trout fillets
Flour for coating
Salt and pepper to taste
1/2 cup (1 stick) butter
8 ounces slivered almonds, toasted
1 to 2 tablespoons fresh lemon juice

Dip the trout in flour to coat on both sides. Season with salt and pepper. Heat the butter in a 12-inch skillet until the butter is melted and the sizzling stops. Fry the trout in the hot butter until golden brown on both sides. Remove to a platter and keep warm. Sauté the toasted almonds in the pan drippings for 1 to 2 minutes. Deglaze the pan with the lemon juice, stirring constantly. Pour the almond mixture over the trout and serve.

*Yield: 4 servings*

## THAI DIPPING SAUCE

1/3 cup fresh lime juice

3 tablespoons soy sauce

1 tablespoon fish sauce

2 teaspoons sugar

1 teaspoon minced jalapeño chile

## SEARED AHI TUNA

1 tablespoon cracked white
   peppercorns

1 tablespoon sesame seeds

1 teaspoon kosher salt

4 ahi tuna steaks
   (sushi quality is recommended)

Vegetable oil for brushing

**For the sauce**, combine the lime juice, soy sauce, fish sauce, sugar and jalapeño chile in a bowl and mix well. Divide evenly among 4 small bowls.

**For the tuna**, combine the white peppercorns, sesame seeds and kosher salt in a small sauté pan. Cook over medium heat for 5 minutes, shaking the pan occasionally. Brush both sides of the tuna steaks with oil. Apply the sesame seed rub to both sides of the tuna. Grill the tuna over high heat for 3 to 4 minutes, turning once. Serve with the dipping sauce.

*Yield: 4 servings*

*Local Interest*

*The allure of the sun and sand can be very strong but sometimes can be too much of a good thing. If you become sunburned, relief can be as close as your kitchen. Most people know about the soothing power of the aloe plant, but plain yogurt applied to tender skin can also bring relief. A paste of baking soda and water is also effective. Or try soaking in a bath of lemon juice and wine vinegar or milk. Be sure to drink plenty of water, and in no time you will be back on the beach.*

# Yellowfin Tuna

## SOY GINGER SAUCE

3/4 cup soy sauce

3/4 cup water

1/2 cup rice vinegar

1 ounce minced garlic

1 ounce chopped pickled ginger

## YELLOWFIN TUNA AND SPINACH

2 (8-ounce) yellowfin tuna steaks
(high-grade quality is
recommended)

2 ounces pepper

1 pound spinach, rinsed, stems
removed

1 tablespoon olive oil

1 red bell pepper, julienned (optional)

1/2 cup prepared wasabi (Japanese
horseradish)

*For the sauce*, combine the soy sauce, water, vinegar, garlic and ginger in a bowl and mix well.

*For the tuna*, rub the tuna steaks with the pepper on both sides. Heat a heavy-duty nonstick sauté pan over high heat. Sear the tuna steaks in the pan for 15 to 25 seconds on each side. Remove from the heat. Remove the tuna to a platter or cutting board. Sauté the spinach in the olive oil in the sauté pan over medium heat for a few minutes or until the spinach turns dark green. Do not overcook. Remove from the heat. Divide the spinach evenly among 4 bowls. Slice the tuna steaks very thinly and arrange the slices over the spinach in a star pattern. Spoon 3 tablespoons of the sauce over each serving. Top each with the bell pepper strips and wasabi. Reserve the remaining Soy Ginger Sauce for another use.

*Yield: 4 servings*

# Blackened Fish Fillets

*After fishing aboard the Lucky Stars right out of Sandestin's Baytowne Marina in the Gulf of Mexico, try this recipe for your "catch of the day."*

1/4 cup (1/2 stick) butter, melted
4 (4- to 8-ounce) grouper, snapper, amberjack or dolphin fillets
1 jar Paul Prudhomme's Blackened Redfish Magic
1/4 cup olive oil

1/4 cup (1/2 stick) butter
Butter for sautéing
Sliced green bell pepper to taste
Sliced onion to taste
Fresh lemon juice to taste

Brush 1/4 cup melted butter over the grouper fillets on both sides. Coat the grouper heavily with the Blackened Redfish Magic. Arrange in a shallow dish. Refrigerate, covered, until ready to cook. Heat the olive oil and 1/4 cup butter in a 12-inch cast-iron skillet over high heat until the butter melts and the sizzling stops. Fry the grouper in the hot butter mixture for 5 minutes. Turn the grouper over and fry until done. Remove to a platter and keep warm. Add a small amount of butter to the skillet. Sauté the bell pepper and onion in the butter until tender-crisp. Add lemon juice to deglaze the pan, stirring constantly. Pour the sauce over the grouper and serve.

*Yield: 4 servings*

# Never-Fail Fish

*In Sandestin, simple, healthy food that's easy to prepare and easy to clean up afterwards is always the goal. The title of this recipe says it all.*

4 (4- to 6-ounce) grouper, tilapia or flounder fillets
1/4 cup chopped onion
4 teaspoons chopped fresh parsley
1/4 cup chopped celery

1/2 cup chopped tomato
Salt and pepper to taste
4 teaspoons dry white wine (optional)
Lemon wedges to taste

Arrange each grouper fillet on a buttered sheet of foil large enough to completely enclose the fillet. Combine the onion, parsley, celery and tomato in a bowl and toss to mix. Divide the mixture evenly atop the grouper fillets. Sprinkle with salt and pepper. Pour 1 teaspoon wine over each fillet. Fold or twist the foil around the ingredients to create sealed packets. Grill over hot coals for 5 minutes per 1/2-inch thickness of fish or until the fish flakes easily with a fork. Open the packets carefully, avoiding the steam. Garnish with additional parsley and serve with lemon wedges. You may grill the entire recipe in 1 large foil packet instead of 4 individual packets if desired.

*Yield: 4 servings*

# Baked and Broiled Fish Fillets

2 to 3 pounds white fish fillets
1 cup (2 sticks) margarine, melted
Seasoned bread crumbs to taste
Chopped onion to taste
Parsley flakes to taste

Dip each fish fillet in the margarine to coat. Arrange the fillets on a baking sheet. Top each fillet with bread crumbs, onion and parsley flakes. Pour any remaining margarine over the fillets. Bake at 450 degrees for 6 to 8 minutes. Broil for 1 to 2 minutes or until golden brown. Garnish with fresh lemon wedges.

*Yield: 4 to 6 servings*

# Fried Fish Fillets

2 to 3 pounds white fish fillets
2 to 3 eggs, beaten
Seasoned bread crumbs to taste
Extra-virgin olive oil for frying
Drained capers to taste
White wine to taste
1 tablespoon butter

Dip each fish fillet in the eggs in a shallow dish to coat. Dip in bread crumbs on a plate to coat both sides. Fry the fillets in hot olive oil in a skillet, turning to brown both sides. Add capers, wine and the butter to the skillet. Simmer briefly. Remove from the pan and serve. Garnish with fresh lemon wedges.

*Yield: 4 to 6 servings*

# Crab Imperial

1 pound fresh lump crabmeat, shells removed, flaked
3 tablespoons mayonnaise
2 dashes of Worcestershire sauce
1/2 teaspoon salt
1/8 teaspoon cayenne pepper
1 tablespoon chopped fresh parsley
4 pats of butter
Paprika to taste

Combine the crabmeat, mayonnaise, Worcestershire sauce, salt, cayenne pepper and parsley in a bowl and mix with a fork to avoid breaking the crabmeat lumps. Divide the mixture evenly among 4 baking shells or ramekins. Top each with 1 pat of butter. Sprinkle with paprika. Arrange on a baking sheet. Bake at 375 degrees for 15 minutes.

*Yield: 4 servings*

# Crab Supper Pie

1 cup (4 ounces) shredded Swiss cheese
1 unbaked (9-inch) pie shell
1 (7-ounce) can crabmeat, drained, shells removed, flaked
2 green onions with tops, sliced
3 eggs, beaten
1 cup light cream
1/2 teaspoon salt
1/2 teaspoon grated lemon zest
1/4 teaspoon dry mustard
Dash of mace
1/4 cup sliced almonds

Sprinkle the cheese evenly over the bottom of the pie shell. Top with the crabmeat and sprinkle with the green onions. Combine the eggs, cream, salt, lemon zest, dry mustard and mace in a bowl and mix well. Pour over the prepared layers. Sprinkle evenly with the almonds. Bake at 325 degrees for 45 minutes or until set. Let stand for 10 minutes before slicing and serving.

*Yield: 6 servings*

# Oysters Marseilles

12 slices bacon, chopped
4 garlic cloves, minced
1 cup crabmeat, shells removed, flaked
1/2 cup (1 stick) butter
1/2 cup flour
2 cups chicken broth
Salt and pepper to taste
1/4 cup cream
1/2 cup vermouth
4 1/2 dozen small oysters
1 (14-ounce) can artichoke hearts, drained
Seasoned bread crumbs to taste

Sauté the bacon and garlic in a sauté pan until the bacon is crisp. Remove from the heat. Add the crabmeat and mix well. Set aside. Melt the butter in a saucepan over medium heat. Stir in the flour until smooth. Add the broth gradually, stirring constantly. Cook until thickened, stirring constantly. Season with salt and pepper. Add the cream and vermouth and mix well. Poach the undrained oysters in their own liquid in a pot. Place the artichokes in a buttered baking dish. Spoon the oysters over the top. Spoon the crabmeat mixture over the oysters. Pour the sauce over the top. Sprinkle with bread crumbs. Bake at 350 degrees until bubbly.

*Yield: 4 servings*

## Memories

*Melinda and Gary Knecht first discovered Sandestin in the summer of 1980 when a tropical storm heading for the Texas coast forced them to cancel their reservations on South Padre Island and head in the opposite direction. Since that fateful summer, they have vacationed at Sandestin nearly every year.*

# Chef's Special

4 ounces mixed baby salad greens
8 ounces tuna or red snapper fillets
6 (31- to 35-count) peeled shrimp
6 crawfish tails

6 oysters
Blackening seasoning to taste
Lemon juice to taste
Olive oil to taste

Arrange the salad greens on a plate. Refrigerate, covered, until ready to serve. Season the tuna, shrimp, crawfish tails and oysters with blackening seasoning. Heat a cast-iron skillet over high heat. Add the fish and cook for 60 seconds on each side. Add the shrimp and crawfish tails and cook for 60 seconds. Add the oysters and cook for 60 seconds. Arrange the blackened fish and shellfish on the salad greens. Serve with lemon juice and olive oil.

*Yield: 1 or 2 servings*

 *Poppy's Seafood Factory*

# Blackened Lobster

2 large onions, cut into quarters
4 ribs celery, cut into chunks
2 garlic bulbs, cut into halves
3 large lemons, cut into halves
1 cup salt
1/4 cup cayenne pepper

2 tablespoons black pepper
4 bay leaves
3 pounds live Maine lobster
Extra-virgin olive oil for coating
1 cup blackening seasoning

Combine the onions, celery, garlic, lemons, salt, cayenne pepper, black pepper and bay leaves in a large stockpot. Fill with water to cover and bring to a boil. Puncture the lobster in several places with a metal skewer. Skewer the lobster tail to prevent the tail from curling during cooking. Add the lobster to the pot as soon as the water begins to boil. Bring the mixture to a second boil. Turn off the heat. Let stand, covered, for 15 minutes. Remove the lobster to a cutting board. Remove the head, claws and tail. Remove the lobster meat from the shells and place in a shallow pan. Coat the meat with olive oil and sprinkle evenly with the blackening seasoning. Heat a cast-iron skillet until it begins to turn gray. Sear the lobster in the skillet for 2 minutes on each side. Place the lobster head in the center of a serving plate. Surround the head with the seared lobster pieces. Serve with corn on the cob and boiled new potatoes.

*Note:* You may boil the new potatoes with the lobster.

*Yield: 6 servings*

 *Poppy's Seafood Factory*

# Grilled Rock Lobster

## CILANTRO PAPAYA DIPPING SAUCE

1 medium Jamaican papaya, peeled, seeded, coarsely chopped

1 (2-inch) piece fresh gingerroot, grated

1 bunch fresh cilantro, chopped

Juice of 2 limes

1 (6-ounce) can Goya papaya nectar

1 tablespoon One Stop Jamaican jerk sauce

## GRILLED ROCK LOBSTER TAILS

8 (6-ounce) Florida rock lobster tails

1 (6-ounce) bottle One Stop Jamaican jerk sauce

*For the sauce*, combine the papaya, gingerroot, cilantro, lime juice and papaya nectar in a food processor and process at high speed until puréed. Add the jerk sauce, processing constantly. Pour into a serving bowl or 8 individual dipping bowls.

*For the lobster tails*, cut the lobster tails down the center, cutting almost all the way through, but leaving the tails intact. Open the lobster tail to resemble a horseshoe shape and rinse the inside to remove any pieces of shell. Coat each lobster tail with a layer of the jerk sauce. Arrange the lobster tails on a grill rack set over hot coals. Grill for 4 to 5 minutes on each side or until the lobster is cooked through. Remove to a serving platter and serve with the dipping sauce.

*Yield: 8 servings*

# Shrimp Scampi

2 pounds fresh large shrimp
1/2 cup (1 stick) butter
1 teaspoon salt
6 garlic cloves

1/4 cup chopped fresh parsley
3 tablespoons lemon juice
1 teaspoon paprika

Peel the shrimp, leaving the shells on the tails only. Devein the shrimp and rinse under running water. Drain on paper towels. Melt the butter in a baking dish in a preheated 400- degree oven. Add the salt, garlic and 1 tablespoon of the parsley and mix well. Arrange the shrimp in a single layer over the garlic butter mixture. Bake, uncovered, for 5 minutes. Turn the shrimp and sprinkle with the lemon juice, paprika and remaining parsley. Bake for 8 to 10 minutes longer. Do not overcook. Arrange the shrimp on a heated serving platter. Pour the garlic butter mixture over the shrimp. Garnish with lemon wedges.

*Yield: 4 to 6 servings*

# Destin's Barbecued Shrimp

2 cups (4 sticks) butter
2 cups (4 sticks) margarine
6 ounces Worcestershire sauce
1 teaspoon Tabasco sauce
4 teaspoons salt
1/2 cup pepper

1 teaspoon oregano
1 teaspoon rosemary
4 lemons, sliced
1 cup dry white Rhine wine
3 garlic cloves, peeled
8 to 10 pounds unpeeled fresh shrimp

Melt the butter and margarine in a large saucepan over low heat. Add the Worcestershire sauce, Tabasco sauce, salt, pepper, oregano, rosemary, lemons, wine and garlic and mix well. Arrange the shrimp in a large baking dish or 2 medium baking dishes and pour the butter mixture evenly over the top, stirring until the shrimp are covered and coated. Bake at 400 degrees for 15 to 20 minutes or until the shrimp turn pink, turning once. Serve with a salad and crusty bread.

*Yield: 12 to 16 servings*

# Cashew Shrimp Supreme

1 pound fresh medium shrimp, peeled, deveined
4 teaspoons cornstarch
1/4 teaspoon sugar
1/4 teaspoon baking soda
1/4 teaspoon salt
1/8 teaspoon pepper

1/2 cup vegetable oil
1/2 cup chopped onion
1/4 cup chopped red bell pepper
1 small garlic clove, minced
1 cup chopped zucchini
3 1/2 cups cooked rice
3/4 cup cashews

Cut the shrimp into halves lengthwise. Combine the cornstarch, sugar, baking soda, salt and pepper in a medium bowl and mix well. Add the shrimp and toss gently to coat. Let stand for 15 minutes. Heat the oil in a large skillet. Add the shrimp and stir-fry for 3 to 5 minutes. Drain the shrimp, reserving 2 tablespoons oil in the pan. Stir-fry the onion, bell pepper and garlic in the reserved oil. Add the zucchini and stir-fry for 2 minutes. Stir in the shrimp, rice and cashews. Cook over low heat until heated through, stirring constantly. Spoon into a serving dish. Garnish with red bell pepper rings.

*Yield: 4 servings*

# Creamed Shrimp

1/4 cup (1/2 stick) butter or margarine
1/2 cup thinly sliced green onions
2 (3-ounce) cans sliced mushrooms, drained
3 tablespoons flour
1 cup heavy cream

1/2 cup milk
1/4 cup sherry (optional)
1 teaspoon salt
1/8 teaspoon pepper
1 1/2 pounds shrimp, cooked, peeled, deveined

Heat the butter in a heavy skillet over medium heat until melted. Cook the green onions in the hot butter until translucent, stirring constantly. Add the mushrooms and mix well. Sprinkle the flour evenly over the mushroom mixture and mix well. Stir in the cream, milk and wine. Cook over low heat until the mixture thickens, stirring constantly. Season with the salt and pepper. Fold in the shrimp and heat through, stirring frequently. Serve as an appetizer in miniature patty shells or an entrée in large patty shells or spread over melba toast rounds. You may also serve as an entrée spooned over red snapper fillets that have been lightly seasoned with salt and pepper and broiled in butter.

*Yield: 6 to 8 servings (in large patty shells) or 3 to 4 dozen (in miniature patty shells)*

# Shrimp Tomato Dill Casserole

4 large green onions (white and part of the green tops), sliced
1 tablespoon olive oil
1 garlic clove, minced
1 pound fresh shrimp, peeled, deveined
4 plum tomatoes, chopped

4 ounces feta cheese, crumbled
2 eggs, beaten
1/2 cup heavy cream
1 tablespoon chopped fresh dill weed
1/4 teaspoon Tabasco sauce
1/4 teaspoon salt
1/4 teaspoon pepper

Sauté the green onions in the olive oil in a sauté pan until tender. Add the garlic and sauté for 1 minute. Spoon into a greased 2- to 2 1/2-quart baking dish. Scatter the shrimp over the garlic mixture. Sprinkle with the tomatoes and cheese. Combine the eggs, cream, dill weed, Tabasco sauce, salt and pepper in a bowl and mix well. Pour over the prepared layers. Bake at 400 degrees for 17 minutes or until the shrimp are done. Serve over hot cooked orzo pasta.

*Yield: 4 servings*

# Shrimp Étouffée

1 medium onion, finely chopped
1/4 cup chopped green bell pepper
1/2 cup (1 stick) butter or margarine
1 garlic clove, crushed
1 cup white wine
1 pound fresh shrimp, peeled, deveined

Salt and black pepper to taste
Cayenne pepper to taste
1/4 cup fresh lemon juice
Hot cooked white or brown rice

Sauté the onion and bell pepper in the butter in a sauté pan until tender. Add the garlic and mix well. Reduce the heat to very low. Heat the wine in a skillet. Add the shrimp, salt, black pepper and cayenne pepper and stir to mix. Cook until the shrimp turn pink, stirring frequently. Pour the lemon juice over the shrimp. Bring the mixture to a boil. Pour over the onion mixture. Simmer for 5 to 10 minutes or until the flavors have blended. Do not cook longer than 10 minutes. Spoon over hot cooked rice. Serve with a tossed salad and hot garlic bread.

*Note:* You may substitute crawfish for the shrimp in this recipe.

*Yield: 2 to 4 servings*

# Shrimp Elegante

3 pounds fresh large shrimp,
   peeled, deveined
Salt to taste
1/2 cup (1 stick) butter
3/4 cup olive oil
2 cups coarsely chopped onions
3 garlic cloves, crushed
1/4 cup chopped fresh parsley

1 teaspoon oregano
1/2 cup sauterne or other dry white
   wine
1/3 cup Italian salad dressing
1/4 cup water
4 teaspoons chicken bouillon granules
Freshly ground pepper to taste
8 ounces fettuccini

Remove and discard the tails from the shrimp. Butterfly the shrimp. Blanch the shrimp in boiling salted water for 30 seconds. Drain and place the shrimp in a shallow broiler pan. Heat the butter and olive oil in a large saucepan over medium heat until the butter melts. Add the onions, garlic, parsley and oregano. Cook until the onions are translucent, stirring occasionally. Add the wine, salad dressing, water, bouillon and pepper and stir until the bouillon is dissolved. Reduce the heat to low. Cook for 5 minutes, stirring occasionally. Pour over the shrimp. Refrigerate, covered, for 2 hours. Cook the pasta using the package directions; drain. Uncover the shrimp. Broil 4 inches from the heat source for 5 minutes on each side or until done. Serve over the hot cooked pasta.

*Yield: 6 servings*

## Entertaining Hints

*This favorite easy meal is built around steamed shrimp from one of the local fish markets or groceries. This simple, delicious salad can also be served as an appetizer. For lunch, stuff the salad in tomatoes. For happy hour, serve with your favorite crackers—just the thing for watching the golfers finish the last holes of the day, visiting with friends, or just watching the sun set.*

## Shrimp Boil

---

**RED SAUCE**

2 cups ketchup

1/2 cup lemon juice

1 tablespoon horseradish

6 drops of hot red pepper sauce

1 teaspoon celery salt

1/4 teaspoon salt

**BOILED SHRIMP**

3 quarts water

1 (3-ounce) package crab boil

1 small onion, sliced

1 lemon, sliced

1 garlic clove, sliced

1 tablespoon salt

7 pounds jumbo shrimp, heads intact

*For the sauce,* combine the ketchup, lemon juice, horseradish, hot red pepper sauce, celery salt and salt in a bowl and mix well. Refrigerate, covered, until ready to serve.

*For the shrimp,* bring the water to a boil in a large stockpot. Add the crab boil, onion, lemon, garlic and salt and mix well. Cover and return the mixture to a boil. Add the shrimp and return to a boil. Reduce the heat. Simmer, covered, for 5 minutes or until the shrimp are tender. Drain the shrimp and serve with the red sauce on the side.

*Yield: 10 servings*

*Local Interest*

*Sandestin Resort and our on-resort neighbor, the Sandestin Hilton, combine to be one of the largest employers along the Emerald Coast, providing thousands of job opportunities for local residents. Several years ago, Sandestin's Human Resources Department saw a need and established the Sandestin Academy. This award-winning school provides on-the-job training for high school students planning to pursue careers in the hospitality industry. Sandestin Academy is located at Sandestin and operates throughout the school term.*

# Low Country Boil

18 small red potatoes

12 small ears of corn

2 pounds Polish kielbasa, cut into
   1-inch pieces

1 large package Old Bay seasoning

3 pounds fresh shrimp

Boil the potatoes in water to cover in a large stockpot for 5 minutes. Add the corn and boil for 10 minutes. Add the kielbasa and Old Bay seasoning and boil for 5 minutes longer. Add the shrimp and cook for 3 minutes. Drain and serve.

*Yield: 6 to 8 servings*

# Steamed Seafood Bucket

¼ cup chopped celery

¼ onion, chopped

¼ cup chopped garlic

¼ cup salt

2 tablespoons black pepper

2 tablespoons cayenne pepper

2 bay leaves

2 (1-pound) live Maine lobsters

1 pound king crab legs

1 pound snow crab legs

1 pound crawfish

1 pound shrimp

2 blue crabs

2 cans corn on the cob

6 new potatoes

Vegetable oil for coating

Combine the celery, onion, garlic, salt, black pepper, cayenne pepper and bay leaves in a food processor and process until finely ground. Combine the lobsters, crab legs, crawfish, shrimp, blue crabs, corn and potatoes in a large bowl and coat with oil. Pour the ground spice mixture over the seafood mixture and toss to coat evenly. Steam the coated seafood and vegetables in a steamer for 14 minutes. Remove to a serving platter and serve.

*Yield: variable*

*Hammerhead's Bar & Grill*

# Skewered Caribbean Shrimp

¼ cup minced onion

¼ cup pineapple juice

2 tablespoons lime juice

½ cup barbecue sauce

1 large garlic clove, pressed

1 pound fresh large shrimp, peeled, deveined

Hot cooked rice

Lime wedges to taste

Chopped pineapple, papaya and/or mango to taste

Soak 4 bamboo skewers in water to cover in a bowl for 1 hour while preparing the marinade. Combine the onion, pineapple juice, lime juice, barbecue sauce and garlic in a bowl and mix well. Add the shrimp and stir to coat. Let stand for 30 minutes, stirring occasionally. Drain the skewers. Drain the shrimp, reserving the marinade for basting. Bring the marinade to a boil in a saucepan before basting the shrimp.

Thread the shrimp onto the skewers. Arrange the skewered shrimp on a greased grill rack set over hot coals. Grill for 2 to 3 minutes, basting with the marinade. Turn the shrimp over and baste again. Grill for 2 to 3 minutes longer or until the shrimp turn pink. Serve over hot cooked rice with lime wedges and tropical fruit cups containing chopped pineapple, papaya and/or mango.

*Yield: 4 servings*

# Portobello Shrimp Skewers

BALSAMIC MARINADE

1 cup balsamic vinegar

1 tablespoon Dijon mustard

1 tablespoon brown sugar

1 tablespoon Worcestershire sauce

Salt and pepper to taste

PORTOBELLO SHRIMP SKEWERS

4 large portobello mushrooms, cut into
1-inch pieces

1 pound (16- to 20-count) fresh jumbo
shrimp, peeled, deveined

16 cherry tomatoes

*For the marinade*, combine the vinegar, Dijon mustard, brown sugar, Worcestershire sauce, salt and pepper in a bowl and whisk until well mixed.

*For the skewers*, thread each of 16 wooden skewers with 1 mushroom piece, 1 shrimp, 1 tomato and 1 additional mushroom piece. Arrange the skewers in an oblong glass dish. Pour the marinade over the skewers and turn the skewers until all the ingredients are coated. Marinate, covered, in the refrigerator for 30 minutes. Drain the skewers, reserving the marinade for basting. Bring the marinade to a boil in a saucepan before basting the skewers.

Arrange the skewers on a preheated grill rack over an open flame. Grill until the shrimp are cooked, turning and basting occasionally with the reserved marinade. Remove to a serving platter.

*Yield: 4 servings*

# Paella Valenciana

*Paella is the Spanish equivalent of jambalaya. Originally leftovers were used to make a paella, but it is considered a "true" paella only if it contains seafood, chicken, and pork.*

1 chicken, cut up
12 cups water
3/4 cup olive oil
2 chorizo or andouille sausages, sliced
12 ounces pork, cut into bite-size pieces
8 ounces ham or tasso, cut into bite-size pieces
2 1/2 large onions, chopped
5 garlic cloves, chopped
2 green bell peppers, chopped

1 1/2 pounds peeled shrimp
1 pound crawfish meat
2 cans crushed tomatoes
2 (2-ounce) jars chopped pimentos
Saffron threads to taste
5 tablespoons salt
1 pound crab fingers
6 cups uncooked rice
1 cup sherry
10 asparagus spears
1 (8-ounce) can green peas, drained

Boil the chicken in the water in a stockpot until done. Drain, reserving the cooking liquid. Add enough water or canned chicken broth to the reserved liquid to measure 11 cups; set aside. Chop the chicken into bite-size pieces, discarding the skin and bones. Heat the olive oil in an 8- or 9-quart paella pan or shallow pot over medium heat. Sauté the sausages, pork and ham in the hot oil. Add the onions, garlic and bell peppers and sauté until the onions are translucent.

Add the shrimp, crawfish meat and chicken and cook over medium heat for 2 minutes. Add the tomatoes, 1/2 of the pimentos, the saffron and salt and cook for 2 to 5 minutes. Add the crab fingers, rice, wine and reserved liquid and mix well. Arrange the asparagus spears decoratively over the top. Scatter the green peas and remaining pimentos over the asparagus. Cook, covered, over low heat until the rice is done. Do not stir while the rice is cooking.

*Note:* You may cook the paella, after adding the rice, in a preheated 350-degree oven. You may substitute other shellfish or game, such as clams and mussels, for the fish and meats suggested above.

*Yield: 20 servings*

# Bean Caviar

1 (15-ounce) can kidney beans
3 to 5 ribs celery, finely chopped
1/2 green bell pepper, finely chopped
2 to 3 green onions, finely chopped
1 teaspoon prepared mustard
1/2 bottle ketchup
2 sweet pickles
Sweet pickle liquid to taste

Combine the beans, celery, bell pepper, green onions, prepared mustard, ketchup, sweet pickles and sweet pickle liquid in a bowl and mix well. Serve with fish.

*Yield: 4 to 6 servings*

# Brussels Sprouts and Artichokes

*This is quick and easy and pairs well with seafood.*

1 (10-ounce) package frozen brussels sprouts
1 (14-ounce) can artichoke hearts, drained, cut into halves
2/3 cup mayonnaise
1/2 teaspoon celery salt
1/4 cup grated Parmesan cheese
1/4 cup (1/2 stick) margarine, softened
2 teaspoons lemon juice

Cook the brussels sprouts using the package directions; drain. Cut each brussels sprout into quarters. Arrange the brussels sprouts and artichokes alternately in a greased baking dish. Combine the mayonnaise, celery salt, cheese, margarine and lemon juice in a bowl and mix well. Spoon over the vegetables. Bake at 425 degrees for 8 to 10 minutes or until the sauce is golden brown.

*Yield: 6 servings*

# Cabbage and Noodles

1/4 cup (or more) corn oil
1 (3-pound) head cabbage, shredded
1 large onion, grated
Salt and pepper to taste
1 package dumpling noodles, cooked, drained

Heat the corn oil in a sauté pan over medium heat. Sauté the cabbage and onion in the hot oil until the cabbage is tender, adding additional corn oil if the cabbage begins to stick to the pan. Season with salt and pepper. Add the hot cooked pasta to the cabbage mixture and stir to mix. Remove to a serving platter.

*Yield: 6 to 8 servings*

# Copper Pennies

2 pounds carrots, sliced
Salt to taste
1 green bell pepper, sliced into rings
1 onion, sliced, separated into rings
1 (10-ounce) can tomato soup
1/2 cup vegetable oil
1 tablespoon Worcestershire sauce
1 cup sugar
3/4 cup vinegar

Boil the carrots in salted water to cover in a saucepan until fork tender. Drain and place the carrots in a bowl. Let stand to cool. Add the bell pepper and onion. Combine the soup, oil, Worcestershire sauce, sugar and vinegar in a blender and process until smooth. Pour over the carrot mixture and mix well. Refrigerate, covered, for 12 hours. Stir and serve.

*Yield: 6 servings*

# Festive Corn and Broccoli

½ cup (1 stick) butter
1 (11-ounce) can Mexicorn, drained
1 (10-ounce) package frozen chopped broccoli, thawed, drained
1 teaspoon basil
½ teaspoon salt
⅛ teaspoon pepper
⅛ teaspoon garlic powder

Melt the butter in a heavy 2-quart saucepan over medium heat. Add the Mexicorn, broccoli, basil, salt, pepper and garlic powder and stir to mix. Cook, covered, over medium heat for 8 to 10 minutes or until the corn and broccoli are tender-crisp. Remove to a serving bowl.

*Yield: 6 servings*

# Garden Green Beans

1 pound fresh green beans, trimmed
4 slices bacon, cut into ½-inch pieces
1 cup sliced red onion
3 tablespoons butter
½ teaspoon salt
½ teaspoon pepper

Place the green beans and bacon in a 3-quart saucepan with enough water to cover. Bring to a full boil. Reduce the heat to medium. Cook for 20 minutes; drain. Return the green beans and bacon to the pan. Add the onion, butter, salt and pepper and mix well. Cook over medium heat for 5 minutes. Remove to a serving bowl.

*Yield: 6 servings*

# Fried Eggplant Sticks

1 eggplant, peeled
Salt and pepper to taste
2 eggs, beaten
2 cups flour
Vegetable oil for frying

Cut the eggplant into 1/2×2-inch pieces. Sprinkle with salt and pepper. Dip the eggplant in the eggs and roll in the flour to coat. Heat 1 to 2 inches of oil in a deep skillet until very hot. Fry the eggplant sticks in the hot oil until golden brown. Drain well on paper towels. Serve hot.

*Yield: 4 servings*


# Eggplant Casserole

2 cups drained cooked eggplant
12 saltine crackers, crushed
1/4 cup (1/2 stick) butter, softened
1 egg
3/4 cup milk
1/2 teaspoon salt
Shredded sharp Cheddar cheese to taste
Paprika to taste

Mash the eggplant with a fork in a bowl, draining any excess liquid. Add the cracker crumbs, butter, egg, milk and salt and mix well. Pour into a greased baking dish and top with a generous amount of cheese. Sprinkle generously with paprika. Bake at 350 degrees for 30 to 40 minutes or until bubbly.

*Yield: 4 servings*

# Vidalia Onion Casserole

*This makes a great side dish for various meats.*

4 to 6 Vidalia onions, sliced

3 tablespoons butter

2 tablespoons flour

Pepper to taste

3/4 cup beef broth

1/4 cup dry sherry

1 1/2 cups croutons

2 tablespoons butter, melted

1/2 cup shredded Swiss cheese

3 tablespoons grated Parmesan cheese

Sauté the onions in 3 tablespoons butter in a sauté pan until tender. Blend in the flour and pepper until smooth. Add the broth and wine and cook until thickened and bubbly, stirring frequently. Spoon into a baking dish. Toss the croutons with 2 tablespoons melted butter in a bowl. Spoon over the top of the onion mixture. Sprinkle evenly with the Swiss cheese and Parmesan cheese. Bake at 350 degrees until the cheese is melted and the mixture is bubbly. Broil for 1 minute or until the top is brown.

*Yield: (about) 8 servings*

## Local Interest

*Sandestin draws visitors and full-time residents with its temperate weather and sunny days. The average annual temperature is 74 degrees Fahrenheit, and Sandestin enjoys 323 days of sun annually. There are 475 acres dedicated to parkland, 165 acres of nature preserves, including wetlands, and 7.5 acres of dune preserves. Add in 7.5 miles of waterfront, and it is easy to see why there are so many residents, human and wildlife.*

# Cheesy Baked Vidalia Onions

4 small Vidalia onions

2 tablespoons chicken broth

2 tablespoons dry white wine

2 tablespoons Worcestershire sauce

1/2 teaspoon hot red pepper sauce

1 tablespoon Morton Nature's Seasons seasoning blend

1/2 teaspoon garlic salt

1/2 teaspoon lemon pepper

1/4 cup (1/2 stick) butter or margarine

4 ounces Jarlsberg cheese, cubed

Cut a thin slice from the bottom of each onion, forming a flat base for the onions to stand upright. Scoop out a shallow hole in the top of each onion. Arrange each onion on a 12-inch square of heavy-duty foil. Fold each of the 4 sides up around each onion to form a basin for liquid, leaving the tops of the onions exposed. Combine the broth, wine and Worcestershire sauce in a bowl and whisk to blend. Drizzle over the onions. Combine the hot red pepper sauce, seasoning blend, garlic salt and lemon pepper in a small bowl and mix well. Sprinkle 2 tablespoons of the mixture over each onion. Top each with 1 tablespoon of the butter. Press the foil edges together, twisting to seal. Arrange the packets on a baking sheet. Bake at 400 degrees for 1 1/4 hours. Unfold the foil carefully, leaving the onions and liquid in the foil cups. Top each onion evenly with 1/4 of the cheese. Broil 5 1/2 inches from the heat source for 1 to 2 minutes or until the cheese is melted. Serve immediately.

*Note:* Swiss, Monterey Jack with jalapeño chiles or fontina cheese may be substituted for the Jarlsberg cheese.

*Yield: 4 servings*

# Mushroom Casserole

1/2 cup uncooked rice
3/4 teaspoon salt
1 cup boiling water
8 ounces pork, cubed
8 ounces veal, cubed
Shortening for browning
Butter for sautéing
1 1/2 cups chopped celery
3/4 cup chopped onion
1/2 cup chopped green bell pepper
6 ounces whole mushrooms
1 (10-ounce) can cream of mushroom soup
3 tablespoons soy sauce

Combine the rice and salt in a 1 1/2-quart baking dish. Add the boiling water and stir to mix. Cover and set aside. Brown the pork and veal in a small amount of shortening in a skillet. Remove the pork and veal to a plate. Add a small amount of butter to the skillet. Sauté the celery, onion, bell pepper and mushrooms in the hot butter for 5 minutes. Add the sautéed vegetables, browned pork and browned veal to the rice and mix well. Stir in the soup and soy sauce. Bake, covered, at 350 degrees for 1 1/4 hours.

*Yield: 6 servings*

# Easy Spinach Soufflé

6 eggs
16 ounces cottage cheese
2 tablespoons butter, melted
8 ounces American cheese, cubed
6 tablespoons flour
1 (10-ounce) package frozen chopped spinach, thawed, drained
1/8 teaspoon salt

Beat the eggs in a large bowl. Add the cottage cheese and mix well. Add the butter and American cheese and mix well. Add the flour, spinach and salt and mix well. Spoon into an ungreased 9×13-inch baking pan. Bake at 350 degrees for 1 hour.

*Yield: 6 servings*

# Squash Casserole

1 pound summer squash, sliced
1 large onion, chopped
Salt and pepper to taste
6 eggs, lightly beaten
1 cup heavy cream or half-and-half
1 can cream-style corn
1/4 teaspoon salt
1/2 teaspoon Mrs. Dash garlic and herb seasoning
2 tablespoons butter
1 small bunch green onions, finely chopped
1 cup fresh bread crumbs or crushed saltine crackers
Butter

Boil the squash, onion, salt to taste and pepper in water to cover in a saucepan until tender-crisp. Drain and mash lightly. Beat the eggs with the cream in a bowl. Add the corn, 1/4 teaspoon salt and the garlic and herb seasoning and mix well. Melt 2 tablespoons butter in a skillet over medium-high heat. Sauté the green onions in the hot butter. Add to the egg mixture and mix well. Add the squash mixture and mix well. Pour into a well-greased baking dish. Combine the bread crumbs with a small amount of butter in a bowl and toss to coat. Sprinkle evenly over the top. Dot with additional butter. Bake at 350 degrees for 1 hour or until firm.

*Yield: 8 servings*

# Zucchini and Onions

1 onion, sliced
1/4 cup (1/2 stick) butter
6 small zucchini, sliced
1/4 teaspoon salt
1/8 teaspoon pepper
1/2 cup grated Parmesan cheese

Sauté the onion in the butter in a skillet until tender but not brown. Add the zucchini, salt and pepper and cook for 5 minutes, tossing frequently. Add the cheese just before serving and toss to coat well.

*Yield: 6 servings*

1 bunch fresh broccoli, cut into bite-size pieces

8 ounces fresh mushrooms, sliced

2 tablespoons butter

1/2 cup mayonnaise

1/2 cup sour cream

1/2 cup grated Parmesan cheese

1 (14-ounce) can artichokes, drained, cut into bite-size pieces

3 tomatoes, sliced

Salt and pepper to taste

1/4 cup (1/2 stick) butter, melted

1/2 cup bread crumbs

Boil or steam the broccoli until tender-crisp; drain. Sauté the mushrooms in 2 tablespoons butter in a skillet until tender. Combine the mayonnaise, sour cream and cheese in a bowl and mix well. Add the broccoli, mushroom mixture and artichokes to the mayonnaise mixture and mix well. Spoon into a greased 9×13-inch baking dish. Layer with the tomatoes. Season with salt and pepper. Combine 1/4 cup melted butter and the bread crumbs in a bowl and toss to coat. Sprinkle evenly over the tomatoes. Bake at 325 degrees for 20 minutes.

*Yield: 10 to 12 servings*

*Local Interest*

*Stuck in the sand? Do you travel on sandy roads and areas of the Emerald Coast without a four-wheel drive vehicle? If so, one day you may return to your vehicle from a nature walk and find it stuck in our wonderful white sand. The first temptation is to try to drive forward. If you find you do not have any forward motion—STOP. You will only get stuck deeper by spinning your wheels. Instead, wedge something firm under the wheels; even stacks of newspapers and periodicals will work. Then back out. Keep your vehicle moving until you are completely free of the sand.*

# Party Potatoes

8 to 10 medium potatoes, boiled, peeled, cubed
1 cup mayonnaise
1 pound Velveeta cheese, cubed
1 cup chopped onion
8 ounces sliced bacon, crisp-cooked, crumbled
Sliced black olives to taste (optional)
Salt and pepper to taste

Combine the potatoes and mayonnaise in a bowl and toss gently to coat. Add the cheese and onion and mix gently. Spoon into a baking dish. Sprinkle with the bacon and olives. Season with salt and pepper. Bake at 350 degrees for 45 minutes.

*Yield: 6 to 8 servings*

# Lemon Potato Wedges

4 to 6 medium baking potatoes
2 tablespoons margarine, melted
1 1/2 teaspoons grated lemon zest
2 tablespoons lemon juice
1 1/2 teaspoons dill weed
Grated Parmesan cheese to taste

Cut each potato into 8 wedges lengthwise. Soak the wedges in cold water to cover for 30 minutes or longer. Drain and pat dry with paper towels. Combine the margarine, lemon zest, lemon juice and dill weed in a bowl and mix well. Brush the margarine mixture evenly over the potato wedges. Arrange the wedges skin side down on a baking sheet sprayed with nonstick cooking spray. Sprinkle evenly with cheese. Bake at 375 degrees for 45 minutes or until the potatoes are tender and light brown.

*Yield: 6 to 8 servings*

# Perfect Mashed Potatoes

4 pounds baking potatoes, peeled
2 teaspoons salt
1 cup (2 sticks) butter, softened
3/4 cup milk or cream, heated
1 teaspoon salt
1/2 teaspoon white pepper
1 teaspoon prepared horseradish
1 tablespoon chopped fresh parsley or chives (optional)
2 tablespoons butter, melted (optional)

Cut each potato into 1/2-inch cubes. Place in a stockpot with enough water to cover. Bring to a boil. Add 2 teaspoons salt. Boil for 25 minutes or until fork-tender; drain well. Beat the potatoes in a mixing bowl at medium speed, adding 1 cup butter gradually. Add the milk gradually, beating constantly until the mixture is of the desired consistency. Add 1 teaspoon salt, the white pepper and horseradish and mix well. Spoon into a heated serving bowl and top with the parsley and 2 tablespoons melted butter.

*Yield: 8 servings*

# Sweet Potato Casserole

3 cups mashed cooked sweet potatoes

1 cup sugar

2 eggs, beaten

2 teaspoons vanilla extract

1/2 cup (1 stick) butter or margarine, melted

1 cup packed brown sugar

1/3 cup flour

1 cup chopped pecans

1/3 cup butter or margarine, softened

Combine the sweet potatoes, sugar, eggs, vanilla and 1/2 cup melted butter in a bowl and mix well. Pour into a greased baking dish. Combine the brown sugar, flour, pecans and 1/3 cup softened butter in a bowl and mix with a fork until crumbly. Sprinkle evenly over the sweet potato mixture. Bake at 350 degrees for 30 minutes or until heated through.

*Note:* For a Thanksgiving Day feast side dish, prepare this casserole 1 day ahead. Refrigerate overnight and bake the following day.

*Yield: 6 to 8 servings*

## Memories

*George Beher will never forget June 13, 1996. He was playing golf in a mixed scramble with Chad Grave, Connie Niehous, and Carolyne Cannon. Number six on Burnt Pine, is situated along a lake and has a sand trap behind the green, and George was 100% focused on his golf game as he approached it. Using a seven-iron he hit the ball, as luck would have it, exactly where he had aimed. The ball landed on the green, rolled about 20 feet, and disappeared. George assumed it rolled into the sand trap, and he grabbed his putter and sand wedge to go look for it after the foursome made their way to the green. While assisting him, Chad made the traditional "Maybe it's in the hole" comment. Chad then walked over to the hole and exclaimed, "It's in the hole, I swear, it's in the hole!" As George reached over to take the ball out of the hole, he heard a round of applause coming from a group at one of the homes across the lake. He stood there for a moment enjoying the recognition that he so deserved for getting a hole-in-one on the most difficult par three in the world. As he accepted congratulations from his partners, he realized that, at that moment, he was Jack Nicklaus.*

## Green Rice

1 cup rice
2 cups water
1/2 onion, chopped
Margarine for sautéing
1 (8-ounce) can sliced water chestnuts, drained
2 (10-ounce) packages frozen chopped broccoli, thawed, drained
1/2 cup half-and-half
1 (10-ounce) can cream of chicken soup
1 cup (4 ounces) shredded sharp Cheddar cheese
1/4 teaspoon pepper

Cook the rice in the water in a saucepan using the package directions; set aside. Sauté the onion in a small amount of margarine in a skillet until tender. Cut the sliced water chestnuts into even thinner slices. Combine the rice, onion mixture, water chestnuts, broccoli, half-and-half, soup, cheese and pepper in a bowl and mix well. Spoon into a greased baking dish. Bake at 300 degrees for 40 minutes.

*Yield: 6 to 8 servings*

## Wild Rice Casserole

1 package Uncle Ben's long grain and wild rice
1/2 cup (1 stick) margarine, softened
1 cup chopped celery
1/2 cup chopped onion
1 small package slivered almonds
1 small can sliced mushrooms
2 (10-ounce) cans beef broth

Combine the rice, margarine, celery, onion, almonds, mushrooms and broth in a bowl and mix well. Pour into a greased baking dish. Bake at 300 degrees for 1 1/2 hours.

*Yield: 6 to 8 servings*

# Oyster Dressing

½ cup chopped celery

½ cup chopped onion

1 bay leaf

¼ cup (½ stick) butter

6 cups herb-seasoned stuffing mix

1 tablespoon snipped fresh parsley

1 pint fresh oysters

2 eggs, beaten

1 teaspoon poultry seasoning

1 teaspoon salt

Pepper to taste

¼ cup (or less) milk

Sauté the celery, onion and bay leaf in the butter in a large sauté pan until tender. Discard the bay leaf. Add the stuffing mix and parsley and mix well. Drain the oysters, reserving the liquid. Chop the oysters. Add the oysters, eggs, poultry seasoning, salt and pepper to the stuffing mixture and mix well. Pour the reserved oyster liquid into a 1-cup measuring cup. Add enough of the milk to measure ⅓ cup. Add enough of the milk mixture to the stuffing mixture to moisten but not saturate. Spoon into a baking pan. Bake at 350 degrees for 45 minutes or until ready to serve.

*Yield: 6 servings*

## Memories

*Christy and P.J. Burke like to spend the holidays surrounded by family and friends. This Oyster Dressing is a tradition in their family. Christy says, "Our Thanksgiving and Christmas just would not be the same without this dressing. P.J. always buys extra oysters so that he can share them with his family and friends while making his special addition to the meal."*

## Beer Biscuits

1 1/2 cups baking mix
1/2 cup sugar
1/2 cup beer

Combine the baking mix, sugar and beer in a bowl and stir with a fork until a soft dough forms. Drop the dough by spoonfuls 2 inches apart onto a greased baking sheet. Bake at 350 degrees for 10 minutes.

*Yield: 8 to 10 biscuits*

## Cream Cheese Biscuits

8 ounces cream cheese, softened
1/2 cup (1 stick) butter, softened
1 cup self-rising flour

Beat the cream cheese and butter in a mixing bowl at medium speed for 2 minutes or until creamy. Add the self-rising flour gradually, beating at low speed just until blended. Fill ungreased miniature muffin cups. Bake at 400 degrees for 15 minutes or until golden brown. Cool on a wire rack.

*Yield: 6 servings*

# Deluxe Corn Bread

*This makes a great accompaniment to soup.*

2 eggs
1 cup buttermilk
1/2 cup vegetable oil
1 (8-ounce) can cream-style corn
1 cup cornmeal
1 tablespoon baking powder
1 1/2 teaspoons salt

Beat the eggs in a mixing bowl. Whisk in the buttermilk, oil and corn. Mix the cornmeal, baking powder and salt together. Add to the egg mixture and mix well. Pour into a greased 8-inch square or round baking pan. Bake at 375 degrees for 30 to 45 minutes or until done.

*Note:* You may add chopped jalapeño chiles to the batter for a Tex-Mex flavor.

*Yield: 6 servings*

# Spoon Bread

*This spoon bread recipe is not like typical corn bread; it has a much creamier consistency.*

1 (8-ounce) package corn muffin mix
1/2 cup (1 stick) margarine, melted
2 eggs, beaten
1 (15-ounce) can cream-style corn
1 cup sour cream

Combine the corn muffin mix and margarine in a bowl and whisk until blended. Add the eggs, corn and sour cream and mix well. Spoon into a 9×9-inch glass baking dish. Bake at 375 degrees for 35 to 45 minutes or until a knife inserted in the center comes out clean or almost clean and the top of the bread is light brown.

*Yield: 6 to 8 servings*

# Dreaming of Dessert

# Chocolate Mousse-Filled Raspberry Torte

**CHOCOLATE MOUSSE FILLING**

16 ounces bittersweet chocolate

1/2 cup (1 stick) butter

3/4 cup egg yolks

1 cup egg whites

1/4 cup sugar

1 cup heavy whipping cream

**CHOCOLATE RASPBERRY TORTE**

1 (3-layer) recipe chocolate cake, baked, cooled

1 cup framboise simple syrup

Seedless raspberry jam to taste

Buttercream icing to taste

**CHOCOLATE GANACHE**

1 cup heavy cream

8 ounces dark chocolate, cut into small pieces

*For the filling*, melt the chocolate in the top of a double boiler over hot but not boiling water, stirring occasionally. Remove from the heat. Add the butter and stir until melted. Add the egg yolks and stir to combine. Beat the egg whites and sugar in a bowl until soft peaks form. Fold into the chocolate mixture gently. Whip the cream in a bowl until soft peaks form. Fold into the chocolate mixture. Set aside.

*For the torte*, trim the crust from each cake layer. Place 1 cake layer on a cake plate and brush with the syrup. Spread a thin layer of jam over the syrup and top with 1/2 inch of the mousse filling. Top with 1 cake layer. Repeat the layers of syrup, jam and mousse filling. Brush 1 side of the remaining cake layer with syrup and place over the prepared layers. Spread the mousse filling over the outside of the torte, filling all the gaps. Refrigerate, covered, until the mousse filling sets. Spread the buttercream icing over the top and side of the torte; cover the torte and refrigerate.

*For the ganache*, bring the cream to a boil in a saucepan, stirring to prevent scorching. Remove from the heat and add the chocolate, stirring until melted. Place the chilled torte on a screen set over a pan. Pour the warm ganache over the torte, forming a smooth coating. Score the torte, indicating serving pieces. Garnish each slice with a fresh raspberry and a chocolate curl.

*Yield: 10 to 12 servings*

*Village Bakery*

# Caramelized Banana Macadamia Nut Torte

## CAKE

1½ cups (3 sticks) butter

10 ounces sugar

10 ounces macadamia nuts

9 ounces white chocolate

8 ounces flour

1¼ tablespoons vanilla extract

20 ounces egg whites

¼ teaspoon cream of tartar

9 ounces sugar

¼ teaspoon salt

## CARAMEL SAUCE

½ cup water

2½ cups sugar

1 teaspoon cream of tartar

1 cup heavy cream

½ cup (1 stick) butter

## TORTE ASSEMBLY

Sliced fresh bananas to taste

Sugar for coating

*For the cake,* cook the butter in a skillet until brown in color with a nutty aroma;. do not allow the butter to burn. Remove from the heat. Let stand to cool. Combine 10 ounces sugar, the macadamia nuts, white chocolate and flour in a food processor and process until finely ground. Add the vanilla to the cooled butter and mix well. Beat the egg whites in a bowl until soft peaks form. Add the cream of tartar, 9 ounces sugar and the salt and beat until stiff peaks form. Fold the macadamia nut mixture into the egg white mixture gently. Fold in the butter mixture. Spread the batter evenly in a greased and floured 12 ×16-inch cake pan. Bake at 325 degrees for 20 to 25 minutes or until the cake tests done. Cool completely in the pan on a wire rack.

*For the sauce,* combine the water, sugar and cream of tartar in a small saucepan and mix well. Cook until the mixture caramelizes and turns amber in color. Heat the cream in a small saucepan until warm. Add the warm cream to the caramelized mixture gradually, stirring constantly. Cook until a hot steam and bubbling caramel reaction happens, stirring constantly. Remove from the heat and add the butter, stirring until the butter is melted and incorporated.

*For the torte assembly,* cut the cooled cake into three 4×16-inch strips. Layer the cake strips together with a thin coating of the sauce and banana slices between the layers. Refrigerate, covered, until serving time. Cut the torte into 2×2-inch cubes, creating 16 portions. Toss each cube in sugar to coat in a bowl. Caramelize the sugared torte cubes with a culinary blowtorch. Serve with ice cream.

*Yield: 16 servings*

*Bake Shop at Sandestin*

# Old-Fashioned Buttermilk Cake

1¹/2 cups (3 sticks) butter, softened
3 cups sugar
6 eggs, at room temperature
1 cup buttermilk

3 cups flour
1 tablespoon vanilla extract
¹/2 teaspoon baking soda

Cream the butter and sugar in a bowl until smooth. Add the eggs 1 at a time, beating well after each addition. Beat in the buttermilk and flour. Add the vanilla and baking soda and mix well. Pour into a large buttered cake pan. Bake at 350 degrees for 1¹/4 hours or until brown. Serve plain or topped with fresh strawberries.

*Yield: 16 servings*

# Dreamy Caramel Icing

*Don't be put off by the use of buttermilk in this icing. It gives the icing a fabulous flavor and texture and works well with everything from layer cakes to jam cakes.*

1 teaspoon baking soda
³/4 cup buttermilk
3 cups sugar
1¹/2 cups (3 sticks) butter or margarine

3 tablespoons light corn syrup
Dash of salt
1 teaspoon vanilla extract

Dissolve the baking soda in the buttermilk in a bowl, stirring to mix. Combine the buttermilk mixture, sugar, butter and corn syrup in a saucepan. Cook over medium heat to 240 degrees on a candy thermometer, soft-ball stage, stirring constantly. Remove from the heat. Add the salt and vanilla and stir until the mixture reaches the desired spreading consistency. Pour or spread the icing over jam cake or any cake of choice.

**Note:** You may use the cold-water method to test for the soft-ball stage if you do not have a candy thermometer.

*Yield: Enough icing for a 3-layer cake*

# Miracle Whip Cake

MIRACLE WHIP CAKE

2 cups flour

2 teaspoons baking soda

1 cup Miracle Whip salad dressing

1 cup sugar

1 cup lukewarm water

1/4 cup baking cocoa

CARAMEL ICING

1/2 cup (1 stick) margarine

1 cup firmly packed brown sugar

1/4 cup cream

1 1/2 cups confectioners' sugar

*For the cake*, sift the flour and baking soda together. Combine the salad dressing and sugar in a bowl and mix well. Add the lukewarm water and baking cocoa and mix well. Add the sifted dry ingredients and mix well. Pour into 2 greased and floured 9-inch cake pans. Bake at 375 degrees for 25 minutes or until the cake tests done. Cool in the pans for 10 minutes. Remove to a wire rack to cool completely.

*For the icing*, combine the margarine, brown sugar and cream in a heavy skillet. Cook over low heat until the margarine is melted, stirring often. Bring to a boil, stirring constantly. Cook for 1 minute or until the brown sugar is dissolved, stirring constantly. Remove from the heat. Pour into a bowl and let stand until lukewarm. Add the confectioners' sugar 1/2 cup at a time, beating until smooth after each addition. Spread the icing between the layers and over the top and side of the cooled cake.

*Yield: 12 servings*

# Pound Cake

1 cup shortening
1/2 cup (1 stick) butter, softened
3 cups sugar
6 eggs
3 cups flour
1/2 teaspoon baking powder
1/2 teaspoon salt
1 cup milk
11/2 teaspoons almond extract
11/2 teaspoons vanilla extract

Cream the shortening, butter and sugar in a bowl until light and fluffy. Add the eggs 1 at a time, beating well after each addition. Sift the flour, baking powder and salt together. Add to the creamed mixture alternately with the milk, mixing well after each addition. Stir in the almond extract and vanilla. Pour into a greased bundt pan. Bake at 325 degrees for 1 hour and 20 minutes. Cool in the pan for 10 minutes. Invert onto a cake plate.

*Yield: 16 servings*

# Never-Fail Pound Cake

1¹/₂ cups (3 sticks) butter, softened
2 cups sugar
3 cups flour
8 eggs, beaten
2 tablespoons vanilla extract
2 tablespoons lemon extract
Confectioners' sugar to taste
Juice of 2 lemons

Cream the butter and sugar in a bowl until light and fluffy. Add the flour to the creamed mixture alternately with the eggs, beating well after each addition. Stir in the vanilla and lemon extract. Pour into a greased bundt pan. Bake at 350 degrees for 45 to 60 minutes or until the cake tests done. Cool in the pan for 10 minutes. Invert onto a cake plate. Add enough confectioners' sugar to the lemon juice in a bowl to make of a glaze consistency, stirring until smooth. Drizzle over the cooled cake.

*Yield: 16 servings*

## Local Interest

*Highlighting Sandestin's golf facilities is the par-72, 6,670-yard U.S.G.A. championship course, Sandestin Links. Its renowned fourth hole is listed as one of the most penalizing in Florida by Golf Magazine, and the first and eighth greens are referred to by Golf Digest as ". . . the lawn for the Taj Mahal."*

# Chocolate Sheet Cake

## CHOCOLATE SHEET CAKE

2 cups flour
2 cups sugar
1/2 teaspoon salt
1 cup (2 sticks) butter
1 cup water
3 tablespoons baking cocoa

2 eggs, well beaten
1/2 cup buttermilk
1 teaspoon baking soda
1 teaspoon cinnamon
1 teaspoon vanilla extract

## CHOCOLATE PECAN ICING

1/2 cup (1 stick) butter
3 tablespoons baking cocoa
6 tablespoons milk
1 (1-pound) package confectioners'
   sugar

1/2 cup chopped pecans
1 tablespoon vanilla extract

*For the cake,* sift the flour, sugar and salt into a heatproof bowl. Combine the butter, water and baking cocoa in a saucepan. Bring to a boil, stirring constantly. Pour over the flour mixture and mix well. Combine the eggs, buttermilk, baking soda, cinnamon and vanilla in a bowl and mix well. Add to the flour mixture and mix well. Pour into a greased and floured 9×13-inch cake pan. Bake at 350 degrees for 20 minutes.

*For the icing,* combine the butter, baking cocoa and milk in a saucepan. Heat until the butter is melted, stirring frequently; do not boil. Remove from the heat. Add the confectioners' sugar, pecans and vanilla and mix well. Pour over the hot cake in the pan.

*Yield: 15 servings*

# German Chocolate Crater Cake

1 cup chopped pecans
1 cup flaked coconut
1 (2-layer) package German chocolate cake mix
1/2 cup (1 stick) butter, softened
8 ounces cream cheese, softened
1 (1-pound) package confectioners' sugar
1 (2-ounce) Milky Way candy bar
3/4 cup evaporated milk

Sprinkle the pecans and coconut over the bottom of a 9×13-inch glass baking dish sprayed with nonstick cooking spray. Prepare the cake mix batter using the package directions. Pour the batter evenly over the coconut. Cream the butter and cream cheese in a bowl until smooth. Add the confectioners' sugar and mix well. Spoon over the cake batter. Bake at 350 degrees for 40 to 45 minutes or until the cake tests done. Microwave the candy bar and evaporated milk in a microwave-safe container on Low until the candy bar is melted, stirring once. Poke several holes in the hot cake with the tines of a fork. Pour the candy bar mixture evenly over the cake. Cool on a wire rack.

*Yield: 15 servings*

## Memories

*Anyone who has spent time at Sandestin forms a strong opinion about which season is the best time to visit. Jennifer and Sam Bunn are no different and feel that fall is the best of all. They say that the weather is great, the crowds are gone, and the beaches are just gorgeous. In fact, it was during a visit in October of 1999 that they decided to find a place of their own. Now they can enjoy the football season on the beach, decked out in their best "Tennessee orange" or "Bulldog maroon" swimwear, tailgating in style.*

# Hershey's Syrup Cake

1/2 cup (1 stick) butter or margarine, softened
1 cup sugar
4 eggs
1 teaspoon vanilla extract
1 cup self-rising flour
1 (1-pound) can Hershey's chocolate syrup

Cream the butter and sugar in a bowl until light and fluffy. Add the eggs 1 at a time, beating well after each addition. Stir in the vanilla. Add the self-rising flour and Hershey's syrup and mix well. Pour into a greased and floured 11×13-inch glass baking dish. Bake at 350 degrees for 35 minutes.

*Yield: 16 servings*

# Kahlúa Cake

1 (2-layer) package chocolate fudge cake mix
2 eggs, beaten
1/2 cup Kahlúa
2 cups sour cream
2 cups (12 ounces) semisweet chocolate chips
1 (4-ounce) package vanilla instant pudding mix
1/4 cup vegetable oil

Prepare the cake mix batter using the package directions. Fold in the eggs, Kahlúa, sour cream, chocolate chips, pudding mix and oil. Pour into a greased bundt pan. Bake at 350 degrees for 50 to 55 minutes or until the cake tests done. Cool in the pan for 10 minutes. Invert onto a serving plate. Cool for several hours before serving.

*Yield: 12 to 16 servings*

*Royal Cake*

ROYAL CAKE

3 tablespoons instant coffee crystals

1/2 cup boiling water

1/2 (2-layer) package devil's food
    cake mix

1/2 (2-layer) package orange cake mix

1 cup water

2 eggs

BRANDY CREAM FROSTING

1/2 cup (1 stick) butter or margarine, softened

1 (1-pound) package confectioners' sugar, sifted

3 tablespoons brandy

1 to 2 tablespoons whipping cream

*For the cake*, dissolve the coffee crystals in 1/2 cup boiling water in a bowl. Combine the coffee mixture, cake mixes, 1 cup water and the eggs in a bowl and mix using the cake mix package directions. Pour into a greased and floured bundt pan. Bake at 350 degrees for 40 minutes. Cool in the pan for 10 minutes. Invert onto a serving plate to cool completely.

*For the frosting*, combine the butter and 2 cups of the confectioners' sugar in a bowl and mix well. Add 2 tablespoons of the brandy and mix well. Add the remaining confectioners' sugar, brandy and the cream, stirring until of the desired spreading consistency. Spread over the cooled cake and serve.

*Yield: 16 servings*

# Festive Berry Cake

## BERRY CAKE

1 tablespoon flour
1 (2-layer) package white cake mix
1 (3-ounce) package strawberry
    gelatin
3/4 cup vegetable oil

1/2 cup water
1/2 cup partially thawed frozen
    strawberries
4 eggs

## STRAWBERRY ICING

1/2 cup (1 stick) butter, softened
1 (1-pound) package confectioners'
    sugar

1/2 cup (or less) thawed frozen
    strawberries

**For the cake**, sprinkle the flour over the cake mix in a mxing bowl. Add the gelatin, oil, water and strawberries and beat until thoroughly mixed. Add the eggs 1 at a time, beating well after each addition. Pour into 2 greased and floured 9-inch cake pans. Bake at 350 degrees for 35 minutes. Cool in the pans for 10 minutes. Remove to a wire rack to cool completely.

**For the icing**, beat the butter in a bowl until light and fluffy. Add the confectioners' sugar gradually, beating until smooth. Add enough of the strawberries to make of the desired spreading consistency, stirring to mix. Spread between the layers and over the top and side of the cooled cake.

*Yield: 12 servings*

*Memories*

*Melinda and Gary Knecht have fond memories of staying in villa 216 on the Fairway. It was a particular favorite of theirs because the large deck on the pond behind the villa was shaded from the afternoon sun. They would always take dessert and coffee out to the deck after dinner and watch the children play while they reminisced about their own childhoods and dreamed of the future.*

# Mandarin Orange Cake

*The ingredients for this cake are usually readily available in one's pantry, which makes this an easy dessert to prepare for unexpected guests.*

1 (2-layer) package yellow cake mix
   (without pudding in the mix)
1 (11-ounce) can mandarin oranges
4 eggs
½ cup vegetable oil
1 (15-ounce) can crushed pineapple
12 ounces frozen whipped topping, thawed
1 (4-ounce) package vanilla instant pudding mix

Combine the cake mix, undrained mandarin oranges, eggs and oil in a mixing bowl and beat at high speed for 2 minutes. Beat at low speed for 1 minute. Pour into 3 greased and floured 9-inch cakes pans. Bake at 350 degrees for 20 to 25 minutes or until a wooden pick inserted in the center comes out clean. Cool in the pans for 10 minutes. Remove to a wire rack to cool completely.

Combine the undrained pineapple, whipped topping and pudding mix in a mixing bowl. Beat at medium speed for 2 minutes. Let stand for 5 minutes or until the mixture is of the desired spreading consistency. Spread between the layers and over the top and side of the cooled cake. Refrigerate, covered, for 2 hours or longer before serving. Store leftovers in the refrigerator.

*Yield: 12 servings*

## Pineapple Cake

**PINEAPPLE CAKE**

2 cups flour

2 cups sugar

2 teaspoons baking soda

2 eggs, beaten

2 (8-ounce) cans crushed pineapple

2 teaspoons vanilla extract

**CREAM CHEESE FROSTING**

8 ounces cream cheese, softened

1/4 cup (1/2 stick) margarine, softened

2 cups confectioners' sugar

2 teaspoons vanilla extract

1/2 cup chopped nuts

*For the cake,* combine the flour, sugar and baking soda in a mixing bowl and whisk to blend. Add the eggs, undrained pineapple and vanilla and mix well. Pour into a greased 9×13-inch cake pan. Bake at 350 degrees for 30 to 40 minutes or until the cake tests done.

*For the frosting,* cream the cream cheese and margarine in a bowl until smooth. Beat in the confectioners' sugar and vanilla. Stir in the nuts. Spread evenly over the hot cake. Refrigerate, covered, until ready to serve.

*Yield: 15 servings*

### Local Interest

*Humans are not the only creatures who call Sandestin home. It is important that we respect our wildlife neighbors. White-tailed deer inhabit our woods and roam our golf courses. Foxes, including one who visits golfers at Burnt Pine, hide in dens and holes. Raccoons, rabbits, opossums, skunks, and bobcats have also been seen in the area. Sandestin security and wildlife officers once spotted a young adult bear, clinging to a limb of a pine tree for several hours before ambling off along Heron Walk Drive and off the property. And, of course, let's not forget the alligators that visit from time to time. This is Florida, after all!*

# Pineapple Upside-Down Cake

1 (8-ounce) can sliced pineapple

3 tablespoons butter, melted

1/2 cup packed brown sugar

4 maraschino cherries, cut into halves

1/3 cup shortening

1/2 cup sugar

1 egg

1 teaspoon vanilla extract

1 cup flour, sifted

1 1/4 teaspoons baking powder

1/4 teaspoon salt

Drain the pineapple, reserving the syrup. Cut the pineapple slices into halves or semicircles. Combine the butter, brown sugar and 1 tablespoon of the reserved syrup in a small bowl and mix well. Pour into an 8x8-inch cake pan. Arrange the pineapple over the butter mixture and place 1 cherry half in the center of each pineapple half. Add enough water to the remaining reserved syrup to measure 1/2 cup.

Cream the shortening and sugar in a bowl until light. Add the egg and vanilla and beat until fluffy. Sift the flour, baking powder and salt together. Add to the creamed mixture alternately with the reserved syrup mixture, beating well after each addition. Spread over the pineapple in the prepared pan. Bake at 350 degrees for 45 minutes. Cool in the pan for 5 minutes. Invert onto a serving plate. Serve warm.

*Yield: 8 to 10 servings*

# Rum Cake

## RUM CAKE

1 cup coarsely chopped pecans

5 eggs, beaten

1 (2-layer) package yellow cake mix

1 (4-ounce) package French vanilla
   instant pudding mix

1/2 cup vegetable oil

1/2 cup rum

1/2 cup water

## RUM SAUCE

1 cup sugar

1/2 cup (1 stick) butter

1/4 cup rum

2 tablespoons water

**For the cake,** sprinkle the pecans evenly in the bottom of a greased tube pan. Combine the eggs, cake mix, pudding mix, oil, rum and water in a bowl and beat until well blended. Pour over the pecans in the prepared pan. Bake at 300 degrees for 1 hour and 10 minutes.

**For the sauce,** bring the sugar, butter, rum and water to a boil in a saucepan. Cook until the butter is melted and the sugar is dissolved, stirring constantly. Poke several holes in the hot cake with an ice pick. Pour the sauce evenly over the cake in the pan. Cool on a wire rack for 10 minutes. Invert onto a serving plate.

*Yield: 16 servings*

# Fancy Cake Topping

1 cup sugar
2 tablespoons flour
1 tablespoon cornstarch
Pinch of salt
1 teaspoon butter

1½ cups water
2 (8-ounce) packages chopped
   dates, minced
1 (8-ounce) can crushed pineapple

Combine the sugar, flour, cornstarch, salt, butter, water, dates and pineapple in a saucepan and mix well. Cook until the mixture is thick, stirring frequently. Use to top any cake.

*Note:* This is best prepared 1 day ahead and is especially good on chocolate cake topped with whipped cream.

*Yield: 4 cups (about) topping*

# Lemon Squares

½ cup (1 stick) butter, softened
1 tablespoon sugar
1 cup flour
½ cup chopped pecans
8 ounces cream cheese, softened

1 cup confectioners' sugar
8 to 12 ounces frozen whipped
   topping, thawed
2 (3-ounce) packages lemon gelatin
2¾ cups milk

Combine the butter, sugar, flour and pecans in a bowl and mix well using two knives. Press over the bottom of a lightly greased 9×13-inch baking pan. Bake at 350 degrees for 15 minutes. Cool on a wire rack. Combine the cream cheese, confectioners' sugar and 1 cup of the whipped topping in a mixing bowl and beat until blended. Spread over the cooled crust. Dissolve the gelatin in the milk in a bowl, stirring to mix. Pour over the prepared layers. Refrigerate, covered, until set. Spread the remaining whipped topping evenly over the top. Cut into squares to serve.

*Note:* For Christmas Pistachio Squares, substitute pistachio gelatin for the lemon gelatin and garnish each serving with a cherry. You may freeze any leftovers.

*Yield: 15 servings*

# Raspberry Lemon Squares

**BUTTER CRUST**

1 cup (2 sticks) butter, softened (no substitutes)

1 cup flour, sifted
1/2 cup confectioners' sugar, sifted

**LEMON TOPPING**

4 eggs
2 cups sugar
1/2 cup lemon juice

1/2 cup flour
1/2 teaspoon baking powder

**RASPBERRY JELLY**

2 (10-ounce) packages frozen raspberries
1/2 cup sugar

1/2 cup water
2 envelopes unflavored gelatin
1/4 teaspoon almond extract

*For the crust*, combine the butter, flour and confectioners' sugar in a bowl and mix well. Press over the bottom of a greased 9×13-inch baking pan. Bake at 350 degrees for 25 minutes or until light brown; do not overbake.

*For the topping*, combine the eggs, sugar, lemon juice, flour and baking powder in a mixing bowl and beat at medium speed for 2 minutes. Pour over the hot crust. Bake for 25 minutes longer. Cool in the pan on a wire rack.

*For the jelly,* purée the raspberries in a blender. Strain through a fine sieve into a bowl to remove the seeds. Add the sugar to the purée and mix well. Combine the water and gelatin in a small saucepan. Let stand to soften. Heat until the gelatin is completely dissolved, stirring constantly. Pour into the raspberry mixture. Stir in the almond extract. Set the bowl into a larger bowl of ice water. Let stand until the raspberry mixture is thickened but not set. Spread over the top of the cooled dessert. Refrigerate, covered, until set. Cut into 3-inch squares. Garnish with piped whipped cream roses.

*Yield: 12 squares*

# Favorite Brownies

## BROWNIES

| | |
|---|---|
| 1/2 cup (1 stick) butter | 3/4 cup flour |
| 1 cup packed brown sugar | 1/2 teaspoon baking powder |
| 2 eggs, beaten | 1/2 teaspoon salt |
| 1 teaspoon vanilla extract | 1 cup (6 ounces) chocolate chips |

## BROWN SUGAR FROSTING

| | |
|---|---|
| 1/3 cup butter, softened | 1/4 cup confectioners' sugar |
| 1/2 cup packed brown sugar | 1/4 teaspoon vanilla extract |
| 1 tablespoon cream | |

**For the brownies,** heat the butter and brown sugar in a saucepan over low heat until melted, stirring to mix. Remove from the heat. Cool slightly. Beat in the eggs and vanilla. Add the flour, baking powder, salt and chocolate chips, stirring until the chocolate chips are partially melted. Pour into a buttered 8x8-inch baking pan. Bake at 350 degrees for 30 minutes. Cool in the pan on a wire rack.

**For the frosting,** combine the butter, brown sugar, cream, confectioners' sugar and vanilla in a bowl and mix until smooth and creamy. Spread over the top of the cooled layer. Cut into squares.

*Yield: 8 to 10 servings*

## Fudge Brownies

1/2 cup (1 stick) margarine, softened

1 cup sugar

4 eggs

1 teaspoon vanilla extract

1 (1-pound) can Hershey's chocolate
   syrup

1 cup flour

1 cup chopped nuts

6 tablespoons butter

6 tablespoons milk

1 1/2 cups sugar

1 cup (6 ounces) chocolate chips

Combine the margarine, 1 cup sugar, eggs and vanilla in a bowl and beat until well blended. Stir in the Hershey's syrup, flour and nuts. Pour into a greased 9×13-inch baking pan. Bake at 350 degrees for 25 minutes or until the brownies pull from the sides of the pan. Combine the butter, milk and 1 1/2 cups sugar in a saucepan. Bring to a boil, stirring constantly. Boil for 30 seconds, stirring constantly. Remove from the heat. Add the chocolate chips, stirring until melted. Spread over the top of the warm brownies. Cut into squares.

*Yield: 15 servings*

## Grandma's Brownies

2 cups flour

2 cups sugar

1/2 cup baking cocoa

2 teaspoons baking powder

1/2 teaspoon salt

1 cup vegetable oil

4 eggs, beaten

1 teaspoon vanilla extract

1 cup chopped nuts (optional)

Confectioners' sugar to taste

Combine the flour, sugar, baking cocoa, baking powder and salt in a bowl and mix well. Add the oil, eggs and vanilla and mix well. Stir in the nuts. Pour into a greased 9×13-inch baking pan. Bake at 350 degrees for 30 to 35 minutes or until the brownies pull from the sides of the pan. Cool in the pan on a wire rack. Sprinkle with confectioners' sugar and cut into squares.

*Yield: 15 servings*

# Caramel Brownies

2 eggs
2 cups packed light brown sugar
2 teaspoons vanilla extract
⅝ cup shortening, melted
1 cup flour
2 teaspoons baking powder
1 teaspoon salt
½ cup chopped pecans

Combine the eggs, brown sugar, vanilla and shortening in a bowl and mix well. Mix the flour, baking powder and salt together. Add to the egg mixture and mix well. Stir in the pecans. Pour into a greased 10×15-inch baking pan. Bake at 350 degrees for 30 minutes. Cool on a wire rack. Cut into squares.

*Note:* The brownies will rise and then fall after being removed from the oven.

*Yield: 20 servings*

# Peanut Butter Brownies

4 ounces unsweetened chocolate

3/4 cup (1 1/2 sticks) butter

2 cups sugar

3 eggs

1 teaspoon vanilla extract

1 cup flour

1 1/2 cups peanut butter

1 teaspoon vanilla extract

3/4 cup confectioners' sugar

4 ounces semisweet chocolate

1/4 cup (1/2 stick) butter

Melt the unsweetened chocolate with 3/4 cup butter in a saucepan over low heat, stirring frequently. Stir in the sugar. Add the eggs, 1 teaspoon vanilla and the flour and mix well. Spread in a greased 9×13-inch baking pan. Bake at 350 degrees for 30 to 35 minutes or until the brownies pull from the sides of the pan. Cool in the pan on a wire rack. Cream the peanut butter, 1 teaspoon vanilla and the confectioners' sugar in a mixing bowl until smooth. Spread over the top of the cooled brownies. Melt the semisweet chocolate with 1/4 cup butter in a saucepan over low heat, stirring frequently. Spread over the peanut butter layer. Let stand until set. Cut into squares.

*Yield: 15 servings*

# Black Walnut Oatmeal Cookies

3/4 cup packed brown sugar
1/2 cup sugar
1 1/4 cups (2 1/2 sticks) butter, softened
1 egg
1 teaspoon vanilla extract
1 1/2 cups flour
1 teaspoon baking soda
3/4 teaspoon salt
1 1/4 teaspoons cinnamon
1/3 teaspoon nutmeg
3 cups rolled oats
2 cups chopped black walnuts
1/2 cup raisins (optional)

Combine the brown sugar, sugar, butter, egg and vanilla in a large bowl and beat until smooth. Mix the flour, baking soda, salt, cinnamon and nutmeg together. Add to the creamed mixture and mix well. Stir in the oats, black walnuts and raisins. Drop by spoonfuls onto a nonstick cookie sheet. Bake at 350 degrees for 10 minutes. Cool on a wire rack.

*Yield: 3 dozen cookies*

## Memories

*Rose and Robert Mannes began coming to Sandestin fifteen years ago, with their then-fourteen-year-old daughter and a AAA Tour Book. Desperate to escape a cold Michigan spring break and in search of sun, sand, and sea, their daughter found an interesting place in the book called Sandestin in Florida's panhandle. Thus began a wonderful adventure for the whole family.*

# Icebox Cookies

2/3 cup butter, softened
1 cup sugar
1 cup packed brown sugar
2 eggs
4 1/2 cups flour
1 teaspoon baking soda
1 cup chopped pecans

Cream the butter, sugar and brown sugar in a bowl until light and fluffy. Add the eggs and beat until well blended. Mix the flour and baking soda together. Add to the creamed mixture and mix well. Stir in the pecans. Divide the dough into 3 equal portions and shape into rolls. Wrap each in waxed paper and freeze until ready to bake. Cut the rolls into thin slices. Arrange on a nonstick cookie sheet. Bake at 350 degrees until light brown. Cool on a wire rack.

*Yield: 4 to 5 dozen cookies*

# Forgotten Cookies

2 egg whites
2/3 cup sugar
1 teaspoon vanilla extract
1 cup chopped pecans
1 cup (6 ounces) semisweet chocolate chips

Preheat the oven to 350 degrees. Beat the egg whites in a mixing bowl until stiff peaks form. Add the sugar gradually and beat at high speed for 5 minutes. Fold in the vanilla, pecans and chocolate chips. Drop by spoonfuls onto a greased cookie sheet. Place in the oven. Turn off the oven immediately. Let the cookies stand in the closed oven for 3 hours or longer. Store in an airtight container.

*Yield: 3 dozen cookies*

# Pecan Finger Cookies

1 cup (2 sticks) butter, softened
1/2 cup confectioners' sugar
1 teaspoon vanilla extract
1 tablespoon hot water
2 cups flour
1/4 teaspoon salt
2 cups finely ground pecans
Confectioners' sugar for coating

Cream the butter, 1/2 cup confectioners' sugar, the vanilla and hot water in a bowl. Add the flour, salt and pecans and mix well. Refrigerate, covered, for 1 hour or longer. Roll the dough into finger-size shapes. Arrange on a nonstick cookie sheet. Bake at 250 degrees until light brown. Roll the hot cookies in confectioners' sugar to coat.

*Yield: 2 to 3 dozen cookies*

## Local Interest

*Attracted by the lovely and massive floral plantings throughout the resort, ruby-throated hummingbirds are a great seasonal favorite. Other species are seen, too, at various times of the year. Large flocks of cedar waxwings devour the holly and yaupon berries in late winter and are easily identified by their buzzing vocalization. Like human vacationers in spring and fall, migratory songbirds also stop in the area for a bit of R and R.*

# Chocolate Chubbies

1 cup (6 ounces) semisweet chocolate chips
2 ounces unsweetened chocolate
1/3 cup butter
3 large eggs
1 cup sugar
1/4 cup flour
1/2 teaspoon baking powder
1/8 teaspoon salt
2 cups (12 ounces) semisweet chocolate chips
3 cups chopped pecans
1 cup chopped walnuts

Combine 1 cup chocolate chips, unsweetened chocolate and butter in a heavy saucepan. Cook over low heat until melted. Remove from the heat. Beat the eggs and sugar in a large bowl until smooth. Beat in the melted chocolate mixture. Combine the flour, baking powder and salt in a medium bowl and stir into the chocolate mixture just until combined; do not overmix. Fold in 2 cups chocolate chips, pecans and walnuts. Drop the batter by spoonfuls 2 inches apart onto a greased cookie sheet. Bake at 350 degrees for 12 minutes. Cool on the cookie sheet for 2 minutes. Transfer to wire racks gently to cool completely.

*Yield: 2 to 3 dozen cookies*

# Peanut Butter Munchies

*This is a family favorite, especially at Thanksgiving and Christmas, that requires just one bowl and no baking!*

1¼ cups graham cracker crumbs
1 cup confectioners' sugar
1 cup creamy peanut butter
¼ cup (½ stick) butter, softened
½ cup chopped walnuts
½ cup flaked coconut
½ cup (or more) confectioners' sugar

Combine the graham cracker crumbs, 1 cup confectioners' sugar, peanut butter and butter in a medium bowl and mix well using a wooden spoon. Shape the mixture into small balls by rolling between your palms. Roll the balls in the walnuts, coconut or ½ cup confectioners' sugar to coat.

**Note:** This recipe is easily doubled, which is good because children and grandchildren quickly devour them.

*Yield: 3 dozen cookies*

## Entertaining Hints

*When unexpected company comes to visit, Sandestin residents Steve and Terrie Mailho have the perfect solution for a casual yet unforgettable outing. Simply grab your favorite picnic hamper and stock it with the makings of a "Sonoma Picnic."*

*Hard Italian salami*
*Sourdough bread (sliced thin)*
*Apples*
*Grapes*
*Cheese, such as pesto Jack and hard Cheddars*
*Wine*
*Small cheese board, cheese knife and cork screw*

*Don't forget the wine glasses!*

# Old-Fashioned Cream Pie

*This is a one-hundred-year-old recipe from Ireland.*

1/3 cup apricot preserves
1 unbaked (9-inch) pie shell
3 tablespoons flour
3 tablespoons (heaping) sugar
Pinch of salt

3 tablespoons clabbered cream (sour)
1 cup heavy whipping cream
1 cup half-and-half
2 egg whites, stiffly beaten
Grated fresh nutmeg to taste

Spread the preserves over the bottom and up the side of the pie shell. Mix the flour, sugar and salt in a bowl. Add the clabbered cream, heavy whipping cream and half-and-half and mix well. Fold in the beaten egg whites. Pour into the prepared pie shell and sprinkle with nutmeg. Bake at 350 degrees for 40 to 50 minutes or until a knife inserted near the center comes out clean. Refrigerate, covered, until thoroughly chilled. Garnish with fresh apricot slices and fresh peppermint leaves.

*Yield: 6 to 8 servings*

# Basic Custard Pie

*This has been a holiday favorite for three generations.*

3 eggs
2 cups sugar
3 tablespoons flour
1/2 cup (1 stick) butter or margarine, melted

3/4 cup evaporated milk
1/4 cup water
1 teaspoon vanilla extract or lemon juice
2 unbaked (9-inch) pie shells

Beat the eggs lightly in a mixing bowl. Add the sugar and flour and mix well. Add the butter and mix well. Add the evaporated milk, water and vanilla and beat until well mixed. Divide the filling evenly between the pie shells. Bake at 400 degrees for 10 minutes. Reduce the oven temperature to 325 degrees. Bake for 25 minutes longer or until slightly firm to the touch.

*Note:* For Sweet Potato Custard Pie, add 1 1/2 cups mashed cooked sweet potatoes and 1 teaspoon cinnamon to the filling ingredients. For Coconut Custard Pie, add 1 cup flaked coconut and 1 teaspoon lemon juice to the filling ingredients. For Chocolate Custard Pie, add 1/4 to 1/3 cup baking cocoa to the filling ingredients. Bake as directed above.

*Yield: 12 to 16 servings*

# Chocolate Chess Pie

1¹/₂ cups sugar
2 tablespoons baking cocoa
2 eggs, beaten
¹/₄ cup (¹/₂ stick) butter, melted
1 teaspoon vanilla extract
1 (5-ounce) can evaporated milk
1 unbaked (9-inch) pie shell
Ice Cream or thawed frozen whipped topping to taste

Combine the sugar, baking cocoa, eggs, butter, vanilla and evaporated milk in the order listed in a mixing bowl and mix well. Pour into the pie shell. Bake at 325 degrees for 40 to 45 minutes or until set. Top each serving with ice cream or whipped topping.

*Yield: 6 to 8 servings*

# Easy Chocolate Pie

2 ounces semisweet chocolate
1 can sweetened condensed milk
¹/₃ cup water
1 teaspoon vanilla extract
1 (9-inch) graham cracker pie shell
2 cups whipping cream
6 tablespoons confectioners' sugar
1 teaspoon vanilla extract

Melt the chocolate in a medium saucepan over low heat, stirring frequently. Add the condensed milk and cook over medium heat for 5 to 8 minutes or until very thick, stirring frequently. Add the water and cook until thick, stirring constantly. Remove from the heat. Stir in 1 teaspoon vanilla. Pour into the pie shell. Refrigerate, covered, until chilled. Beat the cream in a bowl until soft peaks form. Add the confectioners' sugar gradually, beating until stiff peaks form. Fold in 1 teaspoon vanilla. Spoon over the top of the pie. Garnish with unsweetened chocolate curls.

*Yield: 6 to 8 servings*

# Favorite Chocolate Pie

1 bar German's sweet chocolate, finely chopped
1 cup crushed butter crackers
1/2 cup chopped pecans
3 egg whites
1/2 teaspoon vanilla extract
1/2 teaspoon almond extract

3/4 cup sugar
1 teaspoon baking powder
1 cup whipping cream
2 tablespoons sugar
1/2 teaspoon vanilla extract
1/2 teaspoon almond extract

Reserve 2 tablespoons of the chocolate. Combine the remaining chocolate, cracker crumbs and pecans in a bowl and mix well. Beat the egg whites, 1/2 teaspoon vanilla and 1/2 teaspoon almond extract in a bowl until soft peaks form. Combine 3/4 cup sugar with the baking powder in a small bowl and mix well. Add to the egg white mixture gradually, beating until stiff peaks form. Fold the pecan mixture into the egg white mixture gently. Spread over the bottom and up the side of a lightly greased 9-inch pie plate to form a shell. Bake at 350 degrees for 25 minutes or until light brown. Cool on a wire rack. Whip the cream, 2 tablespoons sugar, 1/2 teaspoon vanilla and 1/2 teaspoon almond extract in a bowl until stiff peaks form. Spread in the cooled pie shell. Sprinkle with the reserved chocolate. Refrigerate, covered, for 6 to 8 hours before serving.

*Note:* This can be prepared ahead of time and frozen. Let stand at room temperature to thaw for 1 hour before serving.

*Yield: 6 to 8 servings*

# Microwave Chocolate Pie

*This is a quick yet delicious route to a chocolate cream pie and tastes just like the real deal.*

1 cup sugar
3 tablespoons flour
3 tablespoons baking cocoa
1 cup milk
1/4 cup (1/2 stick) butter, softened
3 egg yolks, beaten
1 teaspoon vanilla extract
1 baked (9-inch) pie shell

Combine 1 cup sugar, flour and baking cocoa in a microwave-safe bowl and mix well. Add the milk and butter and mix well. Microwave on High for 2 minutes. Add the egg yolks and mix well. Microwave on High for 7 to 8 minutes or until thick, beating well at 2-minute intervals. Stir in the vanilla. Pour into the pie shell.

*Note:* You may top with whipped topping before serving.

*Yield: 6 to 8 servings*

# Dutch Apple Pie

5 to 7 tart apples, such as Granny Smith, peeled, sliced
1 unbaked (8- or 9-inch) pie shell
1/2 cup sugar
1 teaspoon cinnamon
1/2 teaspoon nutmeg
2 tablespoons lemon juice
1/2 cup sugar
3/4 cup flour
1/3 cup butter or margarine

Arrange the apples in the pie shell. Combine 1/2 cup sugar, the cinnamon and nutmeg in a bowl and mix well. Sprinkle over the apples and drizzle with the lemon juice. Combine 1/2 cup sugar and the flour in a bowl and mix well. Cut in the butter until crumbly. Sprinkle evenly over the apples to cover. Bake at 400 degrees for 40 minutes or until the topping is brown and the apples are easily pierced with a wooden pick.

*Yield: 6 to 8 servings*

## Entertaining Hints

*For your next dinner party, plan to stagger the times recipes come out of the oven. Write a game plan so that everything isn't coming out of the oven or finishing up at the same time. Before your guests arrive, use sticky notes to label plates and bowls with recipe names. Enlist help in transferring the correct recipe to the correct serving dish.*

# Key Lime Pie

1 (14-ounce) can sweetened condensed milk
3 egg yolks
½ cup Key lime juice
1 (9-inch) graham cracker pie shell
8 to 12 ounces frozen whipped topping, thawed
8 lime wedges

Combine the condensed milk, egg yolks and lime juice in a bowl and blend until smooth. Pour into the pie shell. Bake at 350 degrees for 10 to 12 minutes. Cool on a wire rack for 10 minutes. Refrigerate, covered, until ready to serve. Top with the whipped topping and lime wedges just before serving.

*Yield: 8 servings*

# Pineapple Chess Pie

4 eggs, lightly beaten
2 cups sugar
1 tablespoon flour
1 tablespoon cornmeal
1/4 cup (1/2 stick) butter, melted
1/4 cup milk
1 (8-ounce) can crushed pineapple
1 unbaked (9-inch) pie shell

Combine the eggs, sugar, flour, cornmeal, butter, milk and pineapple in a bowl and mix well. Pour into the pie shell. Bake at 350 degrees for 45 minutes or until the filling is set in the center and light brown.

*Yield: 6 to 8 servings*

# Pineapple Coconut Pie

1/2 cup (1 stick) butter, melted
2 cups sugar
4 eggs
1 (8-ounce) can crushed pineapple, drained
1 (3-ounce) can flaked coconut
1 tablespoon lemon juice
2 unbaked (8-inch) pie shells

Combine the butter, sugar, eggs, pineapple, coconut and lemon juice in a bowl and mix well. Pour into the pie shells. Bake at 300 degrees for 40 to 50 minutes or until set.

*Yield: 10 to 12 servings*

# Rhubarb Pie

3 cups coarsely chopped rhubarb
3 tablespoons flour
1 1/2 cups sugar
3 eggs, well beaten
1/2 teaspoon nutmeg
1 unbaked (9-inch) pie shell
1 tablespoon butter, chopped

Combine the rhubarb, flour, sugar, eggs and nutmeg in a bowl and mix well. Spoon into the pie shell and dot with the butter. Bake at 400 degrees for 10 minutes. Reduce the oven temperature to 350 degrees. Bake for 30 minutes longer.

*Yield: 6 to 8 servings*

## Local Interest

*The entire Emerald Coast has a revered military history. Sandestin Resort and the adjoining areas are surrounded by some of the largest military installations in the free world. Each serves vital areas that contribute to our country's military strength. Eglin Air Force Base is the armament division of the Air Force. Nearby Hurlburt Field is the home of Air Force special operations. To our east and west there is the Naval Air Station in Pensacola, known for the Blue Angels, and Tyndell Air Force Base in Panama City. The Sandestin area also figures into the military story. During World War II, the first rocket testing took place at Four Mile Village near Sandestin. Even today, you can find still-intact cement bunkers and launch sites from that era.*

# Strawberry Pie

1/2 cup (1 stick) butter, softened
1 cup flour
31/2 tablespoons confectioners' sugar
1 cup sugar
1 cup water
3 tablespoons (or more) cornstarch
1/4 cup strawberry gelatin
Pinch of salt
1/2 teaspoon lemon juice
1 tablespoon sugar
3 to 4 cups coarsely chopped fresh strawberries
1 cup whipping cream, whipped

Combine the butter, flour and confectioners' sugar in a bowl and mix until a soft dough forms. Press over the bottom and up the side of a 9-inch pie plate. Bake at 350 degrees for 20 minutes or until light brown. Cool on a wire rack.

Bring 1 cup sugar, the water, cornstarch, gelatin and salt to a rolling boil in a saucepan, stirring constantly. Set aside to cool.

Sprinkle the lemon juice and 1 tablespoon sugar over the strawberries in a bowl. Add to the cooled gelatin mixture and mix well. Pour into the baked piecrust. Refrigerate, covered, until set. Spread the whipped cream over the top of the pie to cover.

*Note:* You may substitute thawed frozen whipped topping for the whipped cream. You may substitute peach or blackberry gelatin for the strawberry gelatin.

*Yield: 6 to 8 servings*

# Peanut Butter Pie

*This is a simple favorite for family get-togethers. The crust makes a great base for any fruit-filled or pudding-filled pie.*

### VERSATILE CRUST

1 1/2 cups flour
2 tablespoons sugar
1/2 teaspoon salt

1/2 cup vegetable oil
2 tablespoons milk

### PEANUT BUTTER FILLING

1/3 cup peanut butter
2/3 cup confectioners' sugar
1 package vanilla or French vanilla
   instant pudding and pie filling mix

8 ounces frozen whipped topping,
   thawed

*For the crust,* combine the flour, sugar and salt in a bowl and mix well. Add the oil and milk and mix well. Press over the bottom and up the side of a 9-inch pie plate. Bake at 400 degrees for 15 minutes. Cool on a wire rack.

*For the filling,* combine the peanut butter and confectioners' sugar in a bowl and mix until crumbly. Reserve 2 tablespoons of the mixture. Spoon the remaining peanut butter mixture into the baked piecrust. Prepare the pudding mix in a bowl using the package directions for pie filling. Add 2 tablespoons of the whipped topping to the prepared pudding. Pour over the peanut butter layer in the piecrust. Top with the remaining whipped topping and sprinkle with the reserved peanut butter mixture.

*Yield: 6 to 8 servings*

# Aunt Elizabeth's Pecan Pie

2 eggs, beaten
2 tablespoons flour
1/8 teaspoon salt
1 cup sugar
1 cup light or dark corn syrup
2 tablespoons margarine
1 teaspoon vanilla extract
1 cup broken pecans
1 unbaked (9-inch) pie shell

Combine the eggs, flour and salt in a heatproof bowl and beat for 1 minute. Bring the sugar, corn syrup and margarine to a boil in a saucepan. Boil for 2 minutes, stirring constantly. Beat the sugar mixture into the egg mixture. Beat in the vanilla and pecans just until mixed. Pour into the pie shell. Bake at 350 degrees for 50 minutes. Serve with vanilla ice cream.

*Yield: 6 to 8 servings*

## Memories

*Marlene Jenkins shares this special recipe for pecan pie, given to her by her Aunt Elizabeth, who owned a restaurant called Chambers in downtown Nashville. It was close to the Ryman Auditorium which was home to the Grand Ole Opry for many, many years. The country music singers and their fans, as well as many locals, were her steady customers. She had home-baked pies, and her pecan pie was desired by most everyone, including Marlene. "I often asked, or should I say, begged, for the recipe" says Marlene. "I finally received it five years after she closed her restaurant." Now people beg Marlene to make the pie.*

# Kahlúa Pecan Pie

6 tablespoons butter, softened
1/2 cup sugar
3 eggs, lightly beaten
Dash of salt
1 cup dark corn syrup
1 tablespoon Kahlúa, or 1 teaspoon vanilla extract
1 1/2 cups broken pecans
1 unbaked (9- or 10-inch) pie shell
1 cup pecan halves

Cream the butter and sugar in a bowl until blended. Add the eggs, salt, corn syrup and Kahlúa and stir until well blended but not fluffy. Stir in the broken pecans. Pour into the pie shell and top with the pecan halves. Bake at 325 degrees for 50 minutes or until a knife inserted near the center comes out clean.

*Note:* Do not substitute for the butter in this recipe.

*Yield: 6 to 8 servings*

# Butter Tarts

1 recipe pie pastry
1 cup packed brown sugar
2 tablespoons butter, softened
2 eggs
1 teaspoon vanilla extract
1/2 cup corn syrup
1 cup small raisins (currants)

Line tart pans with pastry. Combine the brown sugar, butter, eggs, vanilla, corn syrup and raisins in a bowl and mix well. Fill the prepared tart pans 1/2 to 2/3 full. Arrange on a baking sheet. Bake at 400 degrees for 20 minutes or until the filling is firm.

*Yield: variable*

## Local Interest

*White Christmas at Sandestin? Sandestin may be too far south for snow, but thousands, perhaps millions, of white lights transform Sandestin into a holiday showplace each Christmas season. The highlight is the annual "white lights" decorating contest that spurs both individual homeowners and Sandestin neighborhoods into a friendly competition of brilliant displays. Many neighborhoods host decoration parties where residents socialize while draping white lights on crepe myrtles and anyone who stands still for too long. Even the marina is ablaze with lighted boats. Christmas is truly a time of joy and lights at Sandestin.*

# Cranberry Tartlets

*These are so easy to prepare and are quite tasty. They're great for breakfast or as an addition to a nice Sunday brunch.*

3/4 cup (1 1/2 sticks) butter, melted
1 cup flour
3/4 cup sugar
2 eggs, lightly beaten
1 teaspoon vanilla extract
1 1/2 cups dried cranberries
3/4 cup coarsely chopped walnuts, pecans or macadamia nuts

Brush a tartlet pan with a small amount of the butter. Combine the remaining butter, flour, sugar, eggs and vanilla in a bowl and mix well. Stir in the cranberries and walnuts. The batter will be thick. Fill each buttered tartlet cup with about 1/4 cup of the batter. Bake at 325 degrees for 30 to 40 minutes or until golden brown and slightly crusty on top. A cake tester inserted in the center should come out clean. Remove from the pan to a cooling rack. Store cooled tartlets in an airtight container.

*Note:* These taste best when eaten within 48 hours of baking.

*Yield: 12 tartlets*

1 (3-ounce) package butterscotch cook-and-serve pudding mix
1 1/2 cups sugar
1/2 cup evaporated milk
2 tablespoons butter
1 cup chopped pecans
Vanilla extract to taste

Combine the pudding mix and sugar in the top of a heavy double boiler and mix well. Add the evaporated milk and butter. Cook for 4 to 5 minutes, stirring constantly. Cool slightly. Stir in the pecans and vanilla. Drop by spoonfuls onto waxed paper, forming mounds. Let stand until cool.

*Note:* Do not use instant pudding mix in this recipe.

*Yield: 2 dozen pralines*

*Chocolate Pecan Fudge*

1 (12-ounce) can evaporated milk
5 cups sugar
1/2 cup (1 stick) butter or margarine
1 large bag marshmallows
5 cups chopped pecans
2 cups (12 ounces) semisweet chocolate chips
4 ounces unsweetened chocolate, chopped
1 teaspoon vanilla extract

Reserve 2 tablespoons of the evaporated milk. Bring the remaining evaporated milk, sugar and butter to a boil in a saucepan. Boil slowly for 11 minutes, stirring frequently. Add the marshmallows, pecans, chocolate chips, unsweetened chocolate and vanilla and beat well. Add the reserved 2 tablespoons evaporated milk and beat until well blended. Pour into a lightly greased 9×13-inch dish. Refrigerate, covered, until firm. Cut into 1-inch pieces.

*Yield: 117 pieces*

# Chocolate Marshmallow Fudge

4¹/₂ cups sugar

2 tablespoons light corn syrup

¹/₂ cup (1 stick) butter

1 (12-ounce) can evaporated milk

1 to 3 ounces baking chocolate (optional)

2 cups (12 ounces) chocolate chips

6 small plain chocolate candy bars

1 (7-ounce) jar marshmallow creme

3 cups broken pecans

Bring the sugar, corn syrup, butter and evaporated milk to a boil in a saucepan. Boil for 6 minutes, stirring constantly to prevent sticking. Add 1 to 3 ounces chocolate, stirring until melted. Place the chocolate chips and candy bars in a heatproof bowl. Pour the hot sugar mixture over the chocolate in the bowl and beat well. Add the marshmallow creme and beat until well blended. Stir in the pecans. Pour into 2 buttered rectangular dishes. Cool completely before cutting into squares.

*Yield: 5 to 6 dozen squares*

## Memories

*There is a tradition in the Linkside Village called the POETS Society. While some may think this is a quaint little group that gets together to read poetry, nothing could be further from the truth. POETS is actually an acronym for "Piss On Everything Tomorrow is Saturday." It is held one Friday a month at a different resident's home. Everyone brings their beverage of choice, with simple snacks provided by the host. However, in an effort to outdo each other, the spreads have grown more lavish, and some are even themed events. The POETS Society has been a great hit and has allowed neighbors to get acquainted.*

# Cheesecake

*So good, it's sinful!*

## GRAHAM CRUST

1¹/₄ cups finely crushed graham
   crackers

3 tablespoons sugar
6 tablespoons butter, melted

## CREAM CHEESE FILLING

16 ounces cream cheese, softened
1 teaspoon vanilla extract

3 eggs
1 cup sugar

## SOUR CREAM TOPPING

1 cup sour cream
1 teaspoon vanilla extract

3 tablespoons sugar

*For the crust*, combine the graham cracker crumbs and sugar in a bowl and mix well. Stir in the butter and mix well. Press over the bottom and up the side of a 9-inch pie plate. Bake at 375 degrees for 7 minutes. Cool on a wire rack.

*For the filling*, beat the cream cheese in a bowl until fluffy. Beat in the vanilla, eggs and sugar until almost smooth. Pour into the baked crust. Bake at 350 degrees for 25 to 30 minutes. Cool on a wire rack.

*For the topping*, combine the sour cream, vanilla and sugar in a bowl and mix well. Pour over the baked filling. Refrigerate, covered, for 12 hours before serving. Do not freeze.

*Note:* Do not substitute for the butter in this recipe.

*Yield: 6 to 8 servings*

# Fruit-Topped Cheesecake

## CHEESECAKE
4 graham crackers, crushed

4 eggs

1 1/3 cups sugar

32 ounces cream cheese, softened

1 teaspoon lemon extract

1 teaspoon vanilla extract

## FRUIT TOPPING
2 cups sour cream

3 tablespoons sugar

1/2 teaspoon vanilla extract

1 (21-ounce) can cherry, blueberry or strawberry pie filling

*For the cheesecake,* place the graham cracker crumbs in a greased 9-inch springform pan. Tilt the pan until coated with the crumbs. Combine the eggs, sugar, cream cheese, lemon extract and vanilla in the bowl of an electric mixer or food processor and beat or process until smooth and creamy. Pour into the prepared pan. Bake at 350 degrees for exactly 30 minutes; do not bake longer.

*For the topping,* increase the oven temperature to 450 degrees. Combine the sour cream, sugar and vanilla in a bowl and mix well. Spread the topping over the baked cheesecake. Bake for 10 minutes. Cool slightly. Refrigerate, covered, for 3 hours or longer. Spread the pie filling over the top before serving.

*Note:* The cheesecake can be frozen and will also keep in the refrigerator for up to two weeks if properly covered to prevent drying out.

*Yield: 12 servings*

## Kahlúa Trifle

1 (2-layer) package pudding recipe devil's food cake
1¼ cups Kahlúa
8 ounces frozen whipped topping, thawed
8 Heath or Skor candy bars, crushed

Prepare and bake the cake mix using the package directions for a 9×13-inch cake pan. Cool in the pan on a wire rack. Poke holes in the cake with the tines of a fork. Pour the Kahlúa evenly over the cake. Let stand, covered, at room temperature or in the refrigerator for 8 to 10 hours. Crumble the cake. Layer the crumbled cake, whipped topping and crushed candy bars 1/2 at a time in a trifle bowl. Garnish with strawberries or maraschino cherries. Refrigerate, covered, for 2 to 10 hours before serving.

*Yield: 15 servings*

## Chocolate Decadence

1 package family-size brownie mix
1 package chocolate instant pudding mix
16 ounces frozen whipped topping, thawed
6 Heath candy bars, frozen

Prepare and bake the brownie mix using the package directions for a 9×13-inch baking pan. Crumble the brownies in the pan while still hot. Let stand until cool. Prepare the pudding mix in a bowl using the package directions for pie filling. Pour over the crumbled brownies in the pan. Spread evenly with the whipped topping. Break the candy bars into small pieces and sprinkle over the whipped topping.

*Yield: 15 servings*

# Punch Bowl Trifle

1 (20-ounce) can crushed pineapple

1 cup sugar

1 cup chopped nuts

1 (6-ounce) package strawberry gelatin

24 ounces frozen whipped topping, thawed

2 packages frozen strawberries, thawed

2 angel food cakes, torn into small pieces

1 (7-ounce) package flaked coconut

Combine the pineapple, sugar and nuts in a bowl and mix well. Refrigerate, covered, until ready to use. Prepare the gelatin in a large bowl using the package directions. Refrigerate, covered, until soft-set. Add the pineapple mixture and half the whipped topping to the soft-set gelatin and mix gently. Fold in the strawberries. Layer the angel food cake pieces and gelatin mixture 1/3 at a time in a punch bowl. Spread the remaining whipped topping over the top and sprinkle with the coconut.

*Note:* The flavor improves if the trifle is refrigerated overnight.

*Yield: 30 to 40 servings*

## Local Interest

*If you walk Sandestin beaches after dark, you may witness one of Mother Nature's most remarkable sights—the huge loggerhead sea turtle lumbering ashore to nest or tiny loggerhead hatchlings making a mad dash for the sea. Centuries ago, sea turtles numbered in the millions. Now their numbers are greatly reduced, with some species facing extinction. Along South Walton's beaches, a group of local volunteers called Turtle Watch helps locate and protect sea turtle nests. Be a friend at the beach by removing chairs, umbrellas, toys, and other gear from the beach at night and be sure to remove all man-made trash, especially plastic debris. If you live near the beach, you can help by keeping outside lighting to a minimum during the nesting and hatching season. The first turtles come ashore to nest in May and the last hatching usually occurs in October.*

# Schaum Torte

*A delicious summertime treat, this dessert is of German origin, schaum meaning foam in German.*

6 egg whites
2 cups sugar
1 to 1½ teaspoons lemon juice or vinegar
1 teaspoon cream of tartar
1 teaspoon vanilla extract
1 cup whipping cream
1 quart fresh strawberries, hulled, cut into halves, or fresh peach slices

Beat the egg whites in a bowl until soft peaks form. Add the sugar gradually, beating constantly. Add the lemon juice, cream of tartar and vanilla and beat until stiff peaks form. Place in a springform pan. Bake at 275 degrees for 1 hour. Cool in the pan on a wire rack. Remove the top crust from the meringue in pieces and set aside. Whip the cream in a bowl. Add the strawberries and mix gently. Spoon over the meringue in the pan. Arrange the removed meringue pieces back over the top. Refrigerate, covered, until serving time. Place the torte on a serving plate. Loosen the torte from the side of the pan. Remove the side of the pan and serve immediately.

*Yield: 8 to 10 servings*

# Grandma's Fruit Cobbler

*This is good using blueberries or raspberries, but it is especially delicious prepared with the wild dewberries growing in Sandestin in April or with peaches you might get from Chilton County, Alabama, in the summer.*

2 cups fruit, such as blueberries, raspberries,
   dewberries or sliced peaches
1/2 cup sugar
1/2 cup (1 stick) butter
1 cup sugar
3/4 cup flour
2 teaspoons baking powder
Pinch of salt
3/4 cup milk

Combine the fruit and 1/2 cup sugar in a bowl and toss to coat. Let stand for several minutes. Melt the butter in a round glass baking dish in a preheated 350-degree oven. Combine 1 cup sugar, the flour, baking powder, salt and milk in a bowl and stir with a spoon until mixed. Remove the baking dish from the oven as soon as the butter is melted and bubbling. Pour the batter over the butter and top with the fruit mixture; do not stir. The batter will rise to the top. Bake at 350 degrees for 50 to 60 minutes or until brown. Serve plain or with ice cream.

*Yield: 6 servings*

# Bread Pudding

*This is a slight variation of the bread pudding made famous at Bayley's Restaurant in Mobile, Alabama. Just another example of how something really easy can be the centerpiece of supper. The Whiskey Sauce shared below isn't necessary for the bread pudding, but it sure is good!*

### BREAD PUDDING

1 (14-ounce) can sweetened
   condensed milk
3 cups hot water
3 cups (3/4-inch) dry bread cubes
3 eggs, lightly beaten

1 teaspoon vanilla extract
1 tablespoon butter or fat-free spread,
   melted
1/2 teaspoon salt
Ground fresh nutmeg to taste

### WHISKEY SAUCE

6 tablespoons butter
1 cup half-and-half
1 cup sugar

1 egg yolk, beaten
Whiskey to taste

*For the bread pudding,* combine the condensed milk and hot water in a bowl and mix well. Fold in the bread cubes, eggs and vanilla. Add the butter and salt and mix gently. Pour into a 1 1/2-quart baking dish. Place inside a larger baking dish filled with enough hot water to come halfway up the smaller baking dish. Bake at 350 degrees for 1 hour or until the top is golden brown and the pudding is firm but moist. Sprinkle with nutmeg.

*For the sauce,* combine the butter, half-and-half, sugar, egg yolk and whiskey in a heavy saucepan and cook until of the desired consistency, stirring constantly. Serve with the bread pudding.

*Note:* For the best whiskey sauce, mix 4 quarts Black Jack Daniels, Vat No. 7, Sour Mash Whiskey with 15 friends. Stir gently and kick back.

*Yield: 10 to 12 servings*

# Banana Pudding

8 bananas, sliced
Juice of 1 lemon
1 (14-ounce) can sweetened condensed milk
Milk
1 (6-ounce) package vanilla instant pudding mix
Vanilla wafers to taste
8 ounces frozen whipped topping, thawed

Combine the bananas and lemon juice in a bowl and toss gently to coat. Pour the condensed milk into a 4-cup measuring cup. Add enough milk to measure 3 cups and stir to mix. Prepare the pudding mix using the package directions and substituting the condensed milk mixture for the 3 cups milk suggested on the package. Spread a small amount of the pudding in the bottom of a trifle bowl or 9×13-inch dish. Layer with vanilla wafers and the bananas. Fold half the whipped topping into the remaining pudding and pour over the bananas. Top with the remaining whipped topping.

*Note:* The lemon juice not only adds another dimension of flavor to the pudding but also prevents the bananas from turning brown.

*Yield: 12 to 15 servings*

## Entertaining Hints

*Straw baskets filled with blooming plants in small pots make lovely centerpieces. Tuck a little moss around the base of the baskets for a finished look. If magnolias are in bloom, a single blossom floating in a clear or lightly colored glass provides an elegant touch. For a holiday party use the decorations of the season— porcelain bunnies, sprigs of holly or mistletoe, flags— and add greenery for a simple, quick decoration.*

# Lemon Pudding

1 tablespoon butter, softened
3/4 cup sugar
2 tablespoons flour
Juice and grated zest of 1 lemon
2 egg yolks, beaten
1 cup milk
2 egg whites, stiffly beaten

Cream the butter and sugar in a bowl until light and fluffy. Add the flour and mix well. Add the lemon juice and lemon zest and mix well. Add the egg yolks and milk and mix well. Fold in the beaten egg whites. Pour into a well-buttered soufflé dish. Place inside a larger pan filled with 1/4 inch of water. Bake at 325 degrees for 50 to 60 minutes or until puffed and golden brown. Remove to a wire rack to cool. Serve at room temperature or refrigerate, covered in plastic wrap, until serving time.

**Note:** You may, alternatively, prepare the pudding in 31/2-inch individual soufflé dishes to serve as individual snacks. The "soufflé" will fall when removed from the oven.

*Yield: 4 servings*

# Vanilla Tapioca Pudding

3 tablespoons quick-cooking tapioca
1/3 cup sugar
2 cups milk
3 egg yolks
3 egg whites
1 tablespoon vanilla extract

Combine the tapioca, half the sugar, the milk and egg yolks in a saucepan and mix well. Let stand for 5 minutes. Bring to a full boil, stirring constantly. Remove from the heat. Let stand until cool and thick. Beat the egg whites in a bowl until soft peaks form. Add the remaining sugar 1 tablespoon at a time, beating constantly until stiff but not dry. Fold into the cooled tapioca mixture. Stir in the vanilla.

*Yield: 6 servings*

# Chocolate Mousse

1 cup (6 ounces) semisweet chocolate chips
3 tablespoons hot strong brewed coffee
2/3 cup milk, scalded
2 eggs
2 tablespoons rum or orange-flavor liqueur

Combine the chocolate chips, coffee, milk, eggs and rum in a blender and process at high speed for 2 minutes. Pour into 4 dessert cups or demitasse cups and refrigerate, covered, until set.

*Yield: 4 servings*

# Lemon Mousse

3 eggs
1/2 cup sugar
1 teaspoon grated lemon zest
1/2 teaspoon citric acid
1 envelope unflavored gelatin
1/4 cup lemon juice, slightly warmed
2 cups whipping cream, stiffly whipped

Beat the eggs in a bowl. Add the sugar gradually, beating constantly. Add the lemon zest and citric acid and beat until thick and creamy. Dissolve the gelatin in the lemon juice in a small bowl, stirring to mix. Add to the egg mixture and mix well. Fold the egg mixture into the whipped cream. Pour into 6 individual serving dishes. Refrigerate, covered, for 4 to 6 hours before serving.

*Note:* To avoid uncooked eggs that may carry salmonella, we suggest using an equivalent amount of pasteurized egg substitute.

*Yield: 6 servings*

## Frozen Yogurt Pie

16 ounces plain nonfat yogurt
1/2 cup sugar
2 bananas, mashed
8 ounces lite frozen whipped topping, thawed
1 (9-inch) graham cracker pie shell

Combine the yogurt, sugar, bananas and whipped topping in a bowl and mix well. Pour into the pie shell. Freeze until firm.

*Note:* Fruit yogurt may be substituted for the plain yogurt and sugar. Strawberries or other fresh fruit may be substituted for the bananas.

*Yield: 8 servings*

## Frozen Lemonade Pie

1 (14-ounce) can sweetened condensed milk
1 (6-ounce) can frozen lemonade concentrate, thawed
1/2 teaspoon citric acid
12 ounces frozen whipped topping, thawed
1 (9-inch) graham cracker pie shell

Combine the condensed milk, lemonade concentrate, citric acid and whipped topping in a bowl and mix well. Pour into the pie shell. Freeze until firm. Garnish each serving with additional whipped topping and a thin slice of lemon.

*Note:* This will keep well in the freezer for several weeks.

*Yield: 8 servings*

# Frozen Chocolate Dessert

1 package chocolate wafers, crushed
1/4 cup (1/2 stick) margarine, melted
1/4 cup (1/2 stick) margarine, softened
2 cups confectioners' sugar
2 ounces unsweetened chocolate, melted, cooled
1 teaspoon vanilla extract
1/2 cup chopped nuts
3 egg yolks, beaten
3 egg whites, stiffly beaten
1/2 gallon vanilla ice cream, slightly softened

Reserve 2 tablespoons of the wafer crumbs. Combine the melted margarine and remaining wafer crumbs in a bowl and mix well. Press over the bottom of a 9×13-inch pan. Cream the softened margarine, confectioners' sugar and unsweetened chocolate in a bowl until light and fluffy. Add the vanilla and nuts and mix well. Add the beaten egg yolks and mix well. Fold in the beaten egg whites.

Spread the mixture over the crust in the pan. Freeze until firm. Spread the ice cream evenly over the top and sprinkle with the reserved wafer crumbs. Freeze until firm.

*Note:* To crush the chocolate wafers, place in a sealable plastic bag and roll a rolling pin over the bag, or crush in a food processor.

*Yield: 12 to 16 servings*

# Ice Cream Junk

1 to 2 tablespoons butter, melted
1 1/2 cups graham cracker crumbs
1/2 cup (1 stick) butter
3 ounces semisweet chocolate
3 eggs, beaten
2 cups confectioners' sugar
1 teaspoon vanilla extract
1 cup chopped pecans
1/2 gallon vanilla ice cream, softened
Graham cracker crumbs to taste

Combine 1 to 2 tablespoons melted butter and 1 1/2 cups graham cracker crumbs in a bowl and mix well. Press over the bottom of a buttered 9×13-inch pan. Combine 1/2 cup butter and the chocolate in a saucepan. Heat over low heat until melted, stirring frequently. Add the eggs and confectioners' sugar and mix well. Bring to a boil, stirring constantly. Remove from the heat. Add the vanilla and pecans and mix well. Pour over the crust in the pan. Freeze until firm. Spread the ice cream over the top and sprinkle with graham cracker crumbs to taste. Freeze until firm. Cut and serve.

*Yield: 15 servings*

# Peach Melba Ice Cream Pie

1 (3-ounce) can flaked coconut
1/2 cup finely chopped walnuts
2 tablespoons butter, melted
1 quart peach ice cream, softened
1 pint vanilla ice cream, softened
1 (12-ounce) package frozen red raspberries, thawed
1/2 cup sugar
1 tablespoon cornstarch
2 cups sliced peaches, sweetened

Combine the coconut, walnuts and butter in a bowl and mix well. Press over the bottom and up the side of a 9-inch pie plate. Bake at 325 degrees for 10 minutes or until golden brown. Cool on a wire rack. Spoon the peach ice cream into the cooled crust and spread to the edge. Freeze until firm. Spoon the vanilla ice cream over the peach ice cream and spread to the edge. Freeze until firm.

Drain the raspberries, reserving the syrup. Combine the sugar, cornstarch and reserved syrup in a small saucepan. Cook over medium heat until thickened, stirring constantly. Boil for 2 minutes, stirring constantly. Remove from the heat. Stir in the raspberries. Let stand until cool. Arrange the peaches over the top of the pie just before serving. Slice and serve with the raspberry sauce.

*Yield: 6 to 8 servings*

# Homemade Ice Cream

2 cups sugar
1 (14-ounce) can sweetened condensed milk
1 (12-ounce) can evaporated milk
2 teaspoons vanilla extract
3 eggs, beaten

Combine the sugar, condensed milk, evaporated milk and vanilla in a bowl and mix until the sugar is completely dissolved. Add the beaten eggs and mix well. Pour into an ice cream freezer container. Freeze using the manufacturer's directions.

*Note:* Add other ingredients as desired, such as chopped fruit or nuts, before freezing.

*Yield: 1 quart (about)*

# Cinnamon Ice Cream

1 cup sugar
6 tablespoons water
1 1/2 tablespoons cinnamon
3 cups milk
3/4 cup sugar
1 egg, beaten
2 cups whipping cream
1 teaspoon vanilla extract

Combine 1 cup sugar, the water and cinnamon in a saucepan. Cook over low heat until the sugar is dissolved, stirring constantly; set aside. Combine the milk and 3/4 cup sugar in a saucepan and mix well. Scald the mixture. Pour over the beaten egg in a heatproof bowl, beating constantly. Return the mixture to the saucepan. Bring to a boil, stirring constantly. Boil until slightly thickened, stirring constantly. Remove from the heat. Refrigerate, covered, until cool. Stir in the cinnamon mixture. Add the cream and vanilla and mix well. Pour into an ice cream freezer container. Freeze using the manufacturer's directions.

*Yield: 2 quarts*

# Cookies and Cream Ice Cream

5 eggs

2 cups sugar

3 (12-ounce) cans evaporated milk

4 cups milk

2 tablespoons vanilla extract

1 package chocolate sandwich cookies, crushed

Beat the eggs in a bowl until pale yellow. Stir in the sugar, evaporated milk, milk and vanilla and mix until the sugar is completely dissolved. Pour into an ice cream freezer container. Add the crushed cookies. Freeze using the manufacturer's directions or freeze in an old-fashioned crank freezer using rock salt and ice.

*Yield: 4 quarts (about)*

## Entertaining Hints

*A typical day's Sandestin Beach vacation menu might be something like this:*

*Breakfast:*
*Bacon, French toast, orange juice, coffee or milk*

*Lunch:*
*Tuna salad sandwiches, sliced cantaloupe, chips, soft drinks, piña coladas, beer*

*Dinner:*
*Trout Meuniere Almondine or deviled crab, baked potatoes, fresh vegetable medley, salad, rolls, iced sun tea or milk, chocolate mousse*

# Watermelon Sorbet

1 whole seedless watermelon
1/2 cup sugar
1/4 cup honey
1 cup water
8 fresh mint leaves

Remove and discard the rind from the watermelon. Cut the watermelon into large pieces and place in a food processor. Add the sugar, honey, water and mint leaves and process at high speed until completely puréed. Pour into a plastic bowl. Freeze, covered, for 2 to 4 hours or until firm. Scoop into serving dishes and serve.

*Note:* Add sweetener and mint gradually, adjusting for the sweetness of the fruit.

*Yield: variable*

## Entertaining Hints

*Planning a party? The following tips will help keep things sailing smoothly. Plan a menu that you can execute perfectly; this is not the time to experiment. Do all your shopping early and make certain you have all the ingredients you will need on hand. Do as much preparation in advance as possible. That way you will be able to spend time with your guests and enjoy your party. Do not be afraid to accept offers of help, especially at the bar. It takes time to mix drinks and open wine bottles. For a large group it makes sense to hire one or two people to help with serving and clean-up.*

# Speedy Pickled Peaches

1 (20-ounce) can peach halves
Whole cloves to taste
1 (3-inch) stick cinnamon
½ cup vinegar
½ cup sugar

Drain the peaches, reserving the syrup. Stud each peach half with 3 or 4 cloves and arrange in a heatproof dish. Combine the reserved syrup, cinnamon stick, vinegar and sugar in a saucepan and mix well. Simmer for 3 or 4 minutes. Pour over the peaches. Let stand until cool. Refrigerate, covered, for 8 to 10 hours. Serve over vanilla ice cream.

*Note:* You may substitute canned pears in syrup for the peaches in syrup. You may also serve as an accompaniment with poultry, meat or fish dishes.

*Yield: 8 servings*

# Super Fudge Sauce

½ cup (1 stick) butter
1 cup sugar
⅛ teaspoon salt
1 teaspoon instant coffee crystals
2 tablespoons rum
½ cup baking cocoa
1 cup whipping cream
2 teaspoons vanilla extract

Melt the butter in a saucepan over low heat. Stir in the sugar, salt, coffee crystals, rum and baking cocoa. Add the cream and mix well. Bring to a boil, stirring constantly. Reduce the heat and simmer for 5 minutes. Remove from the heat. Stir in the vanilla. Serve warm or cold.

*Yield: 2 cups*

# Chocolate Fondue

6 ounces unsweetened chocolate

1 1/2 cups sugar

1 cup light cream

1/2 cup (1 stick) butter or margarine

1/8 teaspoon salt

3 tablespoons crème de cacao or orange-flavor liqueur

Angel food cake cubes to taste

Pound cake cubes to taste

Apple slices or bite-size pieces to taste

Maraschino cherries to taste

Marshmallows to taste

Melt the chocolate in a saucepan over low heat. Add the sugar, light cream, butter and salt and mix well. Cook for 5 minutes or until thickened, stirring constantly. Stir in the crème de cacao. Pour into a fondue pot and place over the fondue burner. Spear cake cubes, fruit or marshmallows with a fondue fork and dip into the fondue to coat.

*Yield: 6 to 8 servings*

# Homemade Amaretto

1 tablespoon instant coffee crystals
Boiling water
3 1/2 cups sugar
2 tablespoons almond extract
2 dashes of aromatic bitters
1 liter vodka

Dissolve the coffee crystals in a small amount of boiling water in a bowl. Add the sugar, almond extract and aromatic bitters and mix well. Add the vodka and mix well. Let stand until cool.

*Yield: 1 liter*

# Homemade Irish Cream

1 (14-ounce) can sweetened condensed milk
1 cup heavy cream
2 tablespoons Hershey's chocolate syrup
1 cup bourbon whiskey
1 teaspoon vanilla extract
1/2 teaspoon almond extract
1 tablespoon instant coffee crystals

Combine the condensed milk, cream, Hershey's syrup, whiskey, vanilla, almond extract and coffee crystals in a blender and process until well mixed. Pour into a container and cover tightly. Store in the refrigerator for up to 1 month.

*Yield: 3 1/2 cups (about)*

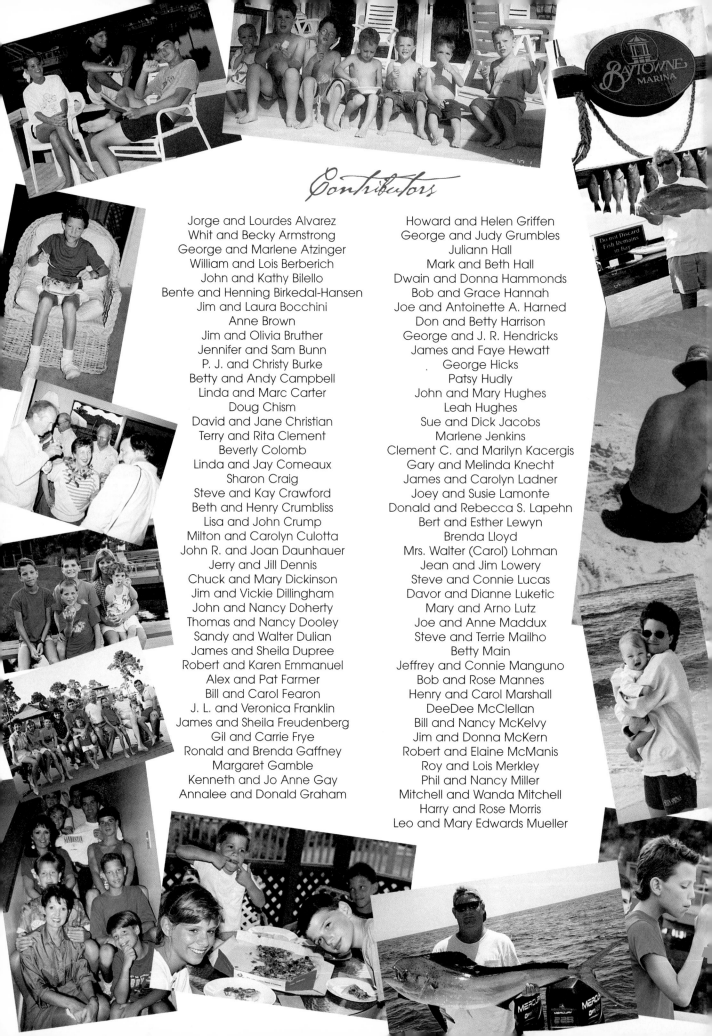

## Contributors

Jorge and Lourdes Alvarez
Whit and Becky Armstrong
George and Marlene Atzinger
William and Lois Berberich
John and Kathy Bilello
Bente and Henning Birkedal-Hansen
Jim and Laura Bocchini
Anne Brown
Jim and Olivia Bruther
Jennifer and Sam Bunn
P. J. and Christy Burke
Betty and Andy Campbell
Linda and Marc Carter
Doug Chism
David and Jane Christian
Terry and Rita Clement
Beverly Colomb
Linda and Jay Comeaux
Sharon Craig
Steve and Kay Crawford
Beth and Henry Crumbliss
Lisa and John Crump
Milton and Carolyn Culotta
John R. and Joan Daunhauer
Jerry and Jill Dennis
Chuck and Mary Dickinson
Jim and Vickie Dillingham
John and Nancy Doherty
Thomas and Nancy Dooley
Sandy and Walter Dulian
James and Sheila Dupree
Robert and Karen Emmanuel
Alex and Pat Farmer
Bill and Carol Fearon
J. L. and Veronica Franklin
James and Sheila Freudenberg
Gil and Carrie Frye
Ronald and Brenda Gaffney
Margaret Gamble
Kenneth and Jo Anne Gay
Annalee and Donald Graham

Howard and Helen Griffen
George and Judy Grumbles
Juliann Hall
Mark and Beth Hall
Dwain and Donna Hammonds
Bob and Grace Hannah
Joe and Antoinette A. Harned
Don and Betty Harrison
George and J. R. Hendricks
James and Faye Hewatt
George Hicks
Patsy Hudly
John and Mary Hughes
Leah Hughes
Sue and Dick Jacobs
Marlene Jenkins
Clement C. and Marilyn Kacergis
Gary and Melinda Knecht
James and Carolyn Ladner
Joey and Susie Lamonte
Donald and Rebecca S. Lapehn
Bert and Esther Lewyn
Brenda Lloyd
Mrs. Walter (Carol) Lohman
Jean and Jim Lowery
Steve and Connie Lucas
Davor and Dianne Luketic
Mary and Arno Lutz
Joe and Anne Maddux
Steve and Terrie Mailho
Betty Main
Jeffrey and Connie Manguno
Bob and Rose Mannes
Henry and Carol Marshall
DeeDee McClellan
Bill and Nancy McKelvy
Jim and Donna McKern
Robert and Elaine McManis
Roy and Lois Merkley
Phil and Nancy Miller
Mitchell and Wanda Mitchell
Harry and Rose Morris
Leo and Mary Edwards Mueller

Peggy Sue Mullins
Roger and Judy Murray
John and Mary Kay Neidhamer
Dale and Barbara Nelson
Leonard and Ruth Nixon
Bev R. and Jeannette Norment
George and Janice M. O'Malley
Shelly Peio
Pat and Joe Persinger
Sandy and Joe Peters
Jo Peterson
John and Nancy Peterson
Ron and Karen Phillips
Vern and Marge Quast
Linda Quinlan
Jean and Jim Rice
Steve and Doris Salzberg
Lawrence and Barbara Sands
Jess and Julie Schroeder
Henry and Shirley Self
Keith and Nicole Sharp
Jack and Ruth Sistrunk
Robert and Sally Stanley
Rod and Vickie Stevens
Merlin and Debbie Stickelber
Gilbert and Pam Stieglitz
Robert and Linda Stone
David and Marilyn Stowe
Jack and Maurine Straub
Jan Strickland
Suzanne and John Sweatt
Joseph and Carole Terry
Beth and Thomas Ventulett
Lamar and Pat Walker
Marg Watkins
Mary Jane Wertz

Caroline and John Williams
Bob and Sharon Wilson
Pat and Gil Winter
Janssen and Hope Woolridge
Harold and Barbara Wright
Harold and Kellie Wright
Roland Yii

*Another Broken Egg Café*
*Bake Shop at Sandestin*
*Beach Club at Sandestin*
*Bijoux Bistro*
*Elephant Walk at Sandestin*
*Hammerhead's Bar & Grill*
*Hilton Hotel's Sandcastles Restaurant*
*Magnolia & Ivy Tearoom*
*Poppy's Seafood Factory*
*Seagar's Prime Steaks & Seafood*
*Sunset Bay Cafe at Sandestin*
*Village Bakery*

*Savoring Sandestin*

Recipes and Memories From Sunrise to Sunset

Sandestin Golf and Beach Resort
Director of Retail Sales
9300 Emerald Coast Parkway West
Sandestin, Florida 32550

| YOUR ORDER | QTY | TOTAL |
|---|---|---|
| *Savoring Sandestin* at $29.95 per book | | $ |
| Postage and handling at $6.95 per book | | $ |
| | TOTAL | $ |

_____
Name

_____
Street Address

_____
City                              State          Zip

_____
Telephone


Payment:  (  )  American Express     (  )  Discover
             (  )  MasterCard     (  )  VISA
             (  )  Check payable to Sacred Heart Hospital on the Emerald Coast


_____
Account Number                    Expiration Date

_____
Cardholder Name

_____
Signature


*Photocopies will be accepted.*